Blood Brother

Blood Brother

JONATHAN DANIELS
and His Sacrifice for Civil Rights

**RICH WALLACE +
SANDRA NEIL WALLACE**

CALKINS CREEK
An Imprint of Highlights
Honesdale, Pennsylvania

For information about
permission to reproduce
selections from this book,
please contact
permissions@highlights.com.

Calkins Creek
An Imprint of Highlights
815 Church Street
Honesdale, Pennsylvania 18431
Printed in China

ISBN: 978-1-62979-094-7

Library of Congress Control
Number: 2016932211

First edition

10 9 8 7 6 5 4 3 2 1

Designed by
Bill Anton | Service Station

Production by Sue Cole
Titles set in Stymie BT Extra
Bold Condensed
Text set in ITC Century Book

For those who marched

in 1965 and those who march today.

"*Be jubilant, my feet!*"

— From *The Battle Hymn of the Republic*
by Julia Ward Howe

Contents

It was their sixth day in hell, otherwise known as the Hayneville jail. Toilets overflowed. Plates of greasy beans rotted on the floor, and the sheriff refused to take any of it away.

"The food is vile and we aren't allowed to bathe," wrote Jonathan Myrick Daniels, dripping with sweat in the hottest week of the summer. There were no fans. Filthy mattresses covered the steel bunks. The water supply to the sinks was frequently shut off.

Yet the jailed protesters were singing. Crammed into four steaming cells, the twenty young people—all but two of them black and most of them teenagers—sang hopeful freedom songs and hymns. Jonathan sang loud and clear, working hard to raise the spirits of his fellow prisoners. The singing was strong enough to be heard three blocks away, increasing the tension in an already riled-up Alabama town.

Oh, Freedom
Oh, Freedom over me
And before I'll be a slave
I'll be buried in my grave,
And go home to my Lord
And be free.

Jonathan was afraid, but he tried to hide it. He'd been warned not to get involved in the protest that landed the group in jail—a peaceful demonstration to call attention to the unfair treatment of black residents at local stores. "They kill people for things like this," a priest told him. "They're looking for people like you."

"People like you" meant white men and women who joined the civil rights movement to help bring about the constitutional freedoms that black people were being denied. In the eyes of many southerners, the only person lower than an African American was any white northerner who came to the South to support the movement. In that summer of 1965, segregationists viewed Jonathan—a twenty-six-year-old white seminary student from New Hampshire—as "a traitor to his own race."

Suddenly the singing stopped. A jailer pulled out his keys and unlocked the cells. "You're free to go," he told the prisoners.

Sidestepping hundreds of paper plates piled high in the hallway reeking of rotting food, the prisoners walked out of jail. But as their eyes adjusted to the sunlight, a wave of fear and suspicion eclipsed their relief. They hadn't been bailed out. Jonathan's friend Stokely Carmichael—a leader of the civil rights organization that was working to raise bail money—was nowhere in sight.

"It didn't feel right," said Ruby Sales. The teenager was convinced that the hasty release was "a setup." They couldn't help thinking about the civil rights workers murdered in Mississippi the summer before. Those three men had been released from jail unexpectedly, too, then shot to death in the middle of the night.

But what could happen in broad daylight on a busy Friday afternoon in Hayneville's town square? Yet it was eerily quiet, the streets deserted.

Deciding that the horrific jail conditions felt safer than walking through Hayneville, Jonathan and the group pleaded to stay on jail property. A deputy sheriff forced them onto the street.

SOMETHING BAD WAS ABOUT TO HAPPEN. RUBY FELT SURE OF IT: "WE WERE LET OUT OF JAIL SPECIFICALLY FOR SOMEONE TO BE KILLED."

Crossing Boundaries

Jonathan and his sister, Emily, are ready to sail on Spofford Lake during a family trip in New Hampshire.

BORN

March 20,
1939

THE FIRST OF
9,651 DAYS

Jonathan Daniels was a rebel, but he was also a deep thinker. As a kid in Keene, New Hampshire, he had a way of discovering secret places where he could sneak away to daydream.

Like that crawl space under his family's house on Summer Street. When he removed the loose bricks from a wall in the basement and grabbed hold of an overhead pipe, Jonathan could swing his feet up and make his way into the space under the dining room. It was cool and dark and smelled like dirt—the perfect meeting place for his friends.

First, it took some work. Jonathan and his friend Bob Perry spent weeks carting out dirt to enlarge the area. "We got on our hands and knees and dug out a bigger space," Bob recalled. Eventually it was eight feet wide and long. They brought in a few old chairs and made a bench with a board and some concrete blocks. But they could dig only at certain times.

"We had to do it when his mother wouldn't be aware," Bob said.

With the space ready, Jonathan assembled his friends in the underground clubhouse. He called his group the Royal Knights of the Order of the Skull and Bones Society. They gathered after school to talk about which girls caught their attention, before turning to deeper subjects. Would the United States' new hydrogen bomb blow up the world? What about the American soldiers fighting in Korea? Jonathan wrote an ominous story about a soldier who came home from the Korean War to find that his family had been killed in a fire.

"DEFIANT AND SNEAKY"

Jonathan's friends knew that he had strict rules to live by. As the son of the town's busiest doctor and a status-conscious mother, he was expected to never bend those rules. Use your best manners at dinner and choose the right silverware. Do your homework and your chores. Always be on time.

Keeping track of time was easy in downtown Keene back in the 1940s and '50s. Train whistles blared at regular intervals, and the Congregational church bell chimed on the hour in the town square.

The difficult part was sneaking around those rules. Clever and resourceful, Jonathan discovered how. By the time he reached junior high school in 1951, twelve-year-old Jonathan Daniels was a firebrand. He'd been "sweet and loving and affectionate and obedient," said his mother. "Suddenly he became argumentative and rebellious and defiant and sneaky." Because Jonathan was constantly grounded, his time with his friends was cut short.

Jonathan was also a bit of a ham. He earned major roles—a wicked magician and Tom Sawyer—in shows put on by the Keene Children's Theater and performed in the school and church choirs and the band. He loved to escape into books, which he said unlocked "a great door to magnificent adventure." The stories that struck him most told about rescues from great danger—the "exciting tales of valiant knights and fair ladies." Thin, klutzy Jonathan "dreamed beautiful, fantastic dreams of myself as a great hero."

He liked to hunker down in the crawl space and light a Camel cigarette—which he kept hidden in an old Band-Aid tin—and listen as his friends described the elaborate ceremonies of their churches. On Sundays, Jonathan, his

Jonathan (at the far right) joined the First Congregational Church youth choir when he was seven years old.

parents, and his younger sister, Emily, attended Keene's First Congregational Church, but he found the services too plain and boring.

Congregationalists "don't kneel and you don't chant and you don't have vestments and all that sort of thing," a friend observed. So Jonathan made his own church. He built an altar in the crawl space and preached sermons to his friends, burning incense and sipping wine he'd swiped from his parents.

Jonathan "wasn't what I would ever call a nerd or odd or anything like that," said a friend. "The idea of being a minister . . . was there growing from the time he was very young."

HAYMAKER PUNCHES

Keene was a busy place. Jell-O boxes, furniture, silver polish, and toys were manufactured in the mills of the small New England city. Elm trees towered above the wide Main Street, and students from Keene Teachers College bustled along the sidewalks.

In the midst of all that busyness stood the white-clapboard Daniels home, just half a block from the library and churches, with schools and the downtown stores another block away.

Though asthma and allergies kept him from being much of an athlete, Jonathan played sports with the neighborhood kids. He even tried to give himself the nickname "Jump," but it didn't stick. Everyone kept calling him Jon or Jonny.

As a Christmas present in eighth grade, Bob Perry received two pairs of boxing gloves, and the Daniels garage became the boxing ring for matches. They put stools in the corners and had a timer for the rounds, and the neighborhood boys gave each other nosebleeds and bruises.

Tall and slight, Jonathan had a boxing style that was frantic and undisciplined. "He was swinging all over the place," Bob said. "It was hard to get through all that flailing." Jonathan took his share of jabs to the jaw, but he knocked a few kids off their feet with wild "haymaker" punches. He was never afraid of challenges, either physical or intellectual.

TIGHT REINS

His friends included kids from all over the city, and Jonathan didn't care if a family was rich or poor or anywhere in between. That didn't always sit well with his mother. Like everywhere else, residents of Keene were acutely aware of class differences. Mill owners and other elites lived in stately mansions along "Millionaires' Row" on Court Street, while the Danielses' neighbors tended to be doctors and other professionals but not rich. There were few black families in Keene, but the city's ethnic and cultural divisions seemed unjust to Jonathan and made him bristle. Some neighborhoods were strictly Irish or Italian, and "If you were an Italian Catholic, you just didn't have anything to do with the people who lived on Court Street," one resident said.

Jonathan crossed all of those boundaries. "I was from the millworkers, and he was from the professionals," said Henry Parkhurst, who became friends with Jonathan during a theater production of *The Wizard of Oz*. Jonathan was comfortable in his poorer friends' homes, where he "liked to be able to sit at a table and eat hot dogs and beans,"

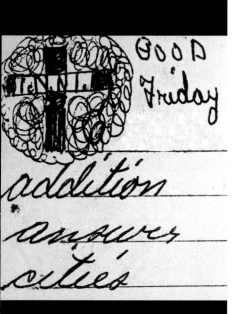

Jonathan sketched this Good Friday cross on a school paper.

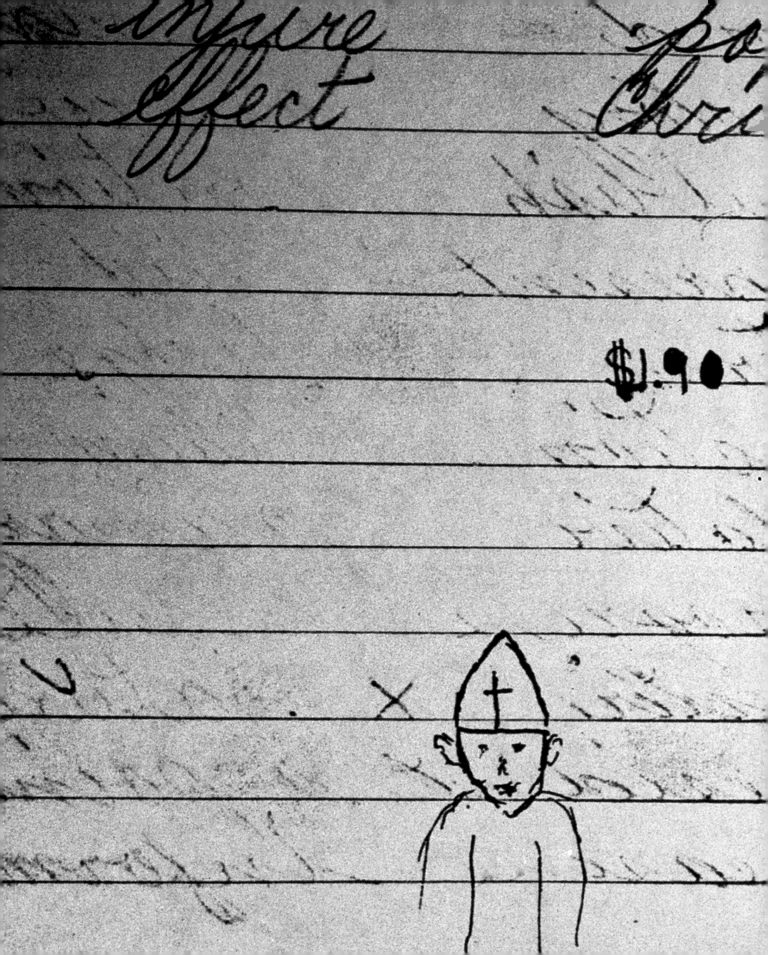

Starting from an early age, Jonathan was fascinated with religious symbols. He drew this bishop on a fourth-grade spelling test.

Parkhurst said. "Nobody was looking to say, 'put your glass a little bit more to the right,' you know, or 'your napkin goes to the left.'"

Dinner at the Daniels home was more like that.

Philip Daniels worked long hours, but he tried to be home for dinner. It was one of the few times of the day that he spent with his wife and two kids. He stayed out late nearly every night, treating patients at his medical clinic or making house calls. Dr. Daniels's devotion to his patients meant missing his kids' homework and bedtimes.

All that extra work didn't bring the family much money either. "Anybody who couldn't afford medical care, immediately the word went out 'call Phil Daniels and he'll come,'" explained daughter Emily, who was four years younger than Jonathan. "If they couldn't get to the clinic he would go to see them."

Friends worried that Dr. Daniels's selflessness put too much strain on his family, but Jonathan never objected. He wrote that his father's "deep concern for human pain . . . shaped my conviction that self-fulfillment lies in service." He learned from Dr. Daniels that "a day's work never ends."

Emily said their mother's role was "to keep an eye on us, and to deal with all the nitpicking social stuff that goes on if you're the wife of a doctor." Connie Daniels spent most evenings at meetings of the League of Women Voters and similar civic groups, or she'd play bridge with other doctors' wives. To the outside world she appeared poised and sophisticated, with pearls and the best manners. But the Daniels home was messy and cluttered. Friends knew to veer to the left when they entered the house, because the right side was piled high with newspapers.

Because his home life wasn't as neat and prosperous as it appeared, Jonathan saw right through any class pretentions. "Jon was able to sit on a torn couch and be comfortable," Parkhurst explained. "Whenever you go in someone's home, they gauge you by the way you are in that home."

Jonathan was well respected in nearly every home he visited. The one where he was judged most sternly was his own.

In this 1953 photo, the First Congregational Church steeple overlooks Keene's wide Main Street.

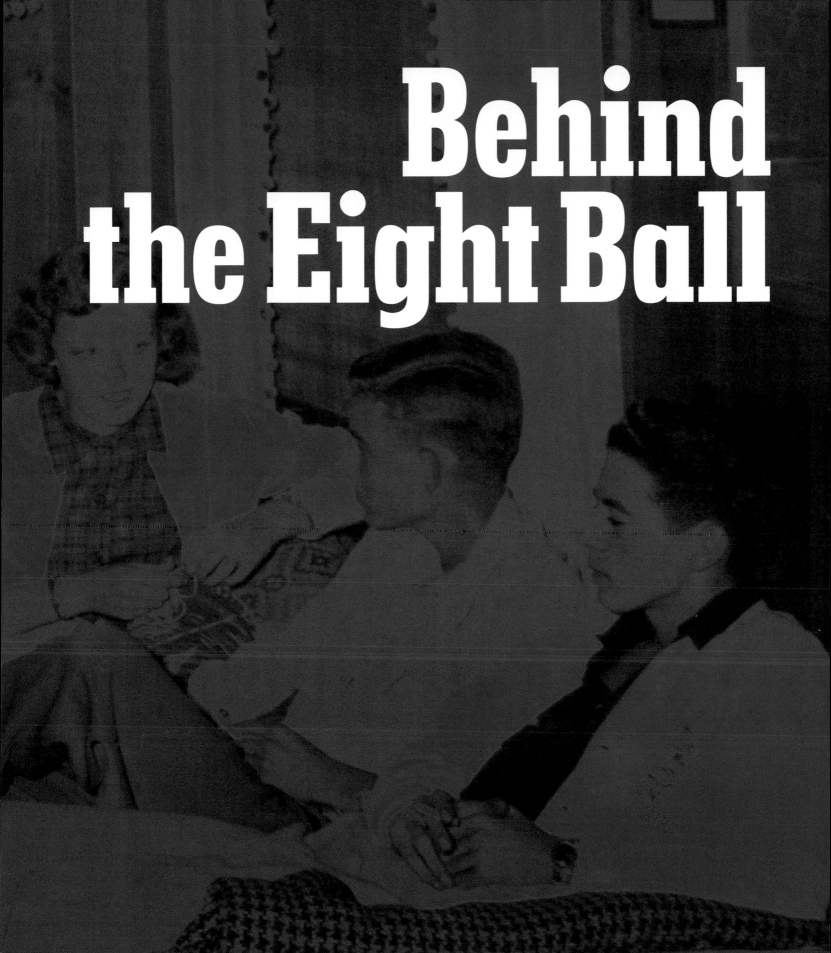

Behind
the Eight Ball

Merry Christmas from the Daniels – 1954

The boards covering the school's broken basement window weren't well secured. Fourteen-year-old Jonathan pried them just enough so he could sneak into the building, then pushed them back into place. He took a deep breath in the dark and tested the floor with his foot.

Jonathan was smart, but he hadn't been a good student at Keene's Central Junior High School. He'd graduated the year before, in 1953, but he couldn't wait to return to the building. Late at night.

Making his way up several flights of stairs to the top floor, Jonathan climbed into the school's bell tower, where he could see out all four sides and have a view of the city. Gazing over at Central Square with its wooded green and the Civil War monument, his view held the steeples of several churches, including the First Congregational Church at the head of the square.

He'd be in trouble if he was caught up there, and his parents would be ashamed of Jonathan and themselves for having a son who broke into buildings. He could fall in the dark, creaky space.

Secretly climbing the tower at night defied his strict upbringing, but it also provided another space for Jonathan to think about where he fit in the world. It gave him room to confront what he called "the Moods"—spells of inferiority and jealousy. He worried about what he would make of his life.

A Daniels tradition: the family Christmas card. Jonathan was a sophomore in high school when this 1954 card was photographed.

The Moods "reached a climax in the ninth grade, where I was submerged in a long period of numerous black fits of depression," he wrote.

Alone with his thoughts above the city, Jonathan weighed his options: Become a doctor like his father? But he was lousy at science. Enter the ministry? He liked helping people. Become a teacher? But how could a poor student be a good educator?

"He went up there many times," said Bob Perry, who joined Jonathan in the tower only once. "It was very dark and we only had one tiny flashlight. We sat up there and had a cigarette. I was afraid someone would see that tiny lit end of the burning cigarette" from down below.

Perry hung back from the edge, counting the minutes until they could leave. Jonathan loved it and returned often, and he climbed into other places he didn't belong—steeples, clock towers, roofs.

That risky climbing landed him in the hospital two years later. By then, he'd found another way to work out his moods: writing for the Keene High School literary magazine, *The Enterprise.* In an essay titled "Reality," Jonathan wrote why he agreed with nineteenth-century philosopher Henry David Thoreau that conveniences and modern advances caused people to lose sight of "the basic fulfillment of our mortal existence."

"Stop, right now, examine your lives," Jonathan urged his fellow students in the essay. "Is life . . . just one long, mad, social whirl?"

Jonathan hoped it wasn't. He'd grown more interested in what people stood for and believed in. A strong, insightful writer, he published dark stories and lighthearted poems,

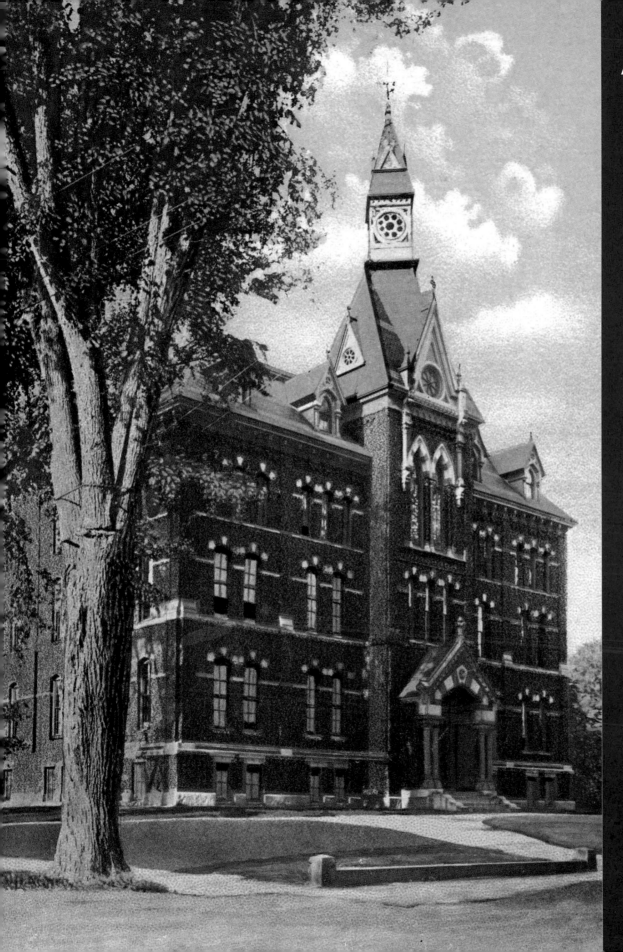

"There wasn't
a steeple
in the city
of Keene that
didn't have
his name,
his initials
carved up
inside there
somewhere."

—a high school friend

The bell tower at
Keene's Central
Junior High School
stood 128 feet
above the ground.
Jonathan climbed up
there often.

27

Jonathan's
lighthearted poem
was published
in Keene High
School's literary
magazine,
The Enterprise.

MERMAID LOVE

JONATHAN DANIELS '57

Down, down, down he strolled,
Down to the edge of the sea.
Out, out, out he swam,
As far as the eye could see.
Down, down, down he dove,
Down to the floor of the sea;
Down and around, up and out,
Chasing his mermaid love.

and he wrote a book-review column for the literary magazine. In one issue, he raved about six books, including works on a World War II hero, an Antarctic expedition, and the sinking of the *Titanic*.

He continued acting like a minister, too. Several times when his girlfriend missed a church service, he visited her home and conducted a service for her. He even gave her a communion wafer.

BEETHOVEN VS. ELVIS

Jonathan's interest in writing led him to become friends with a group of boys who were a year ahead of him in high school. They shared a zany sense of humor and intense interests in acting, religion, and music. Elvis Presley's "Don't Be Cruel/Hound Dog" record held the top spot on the charts for most of the winter of his junior year, but Jonathan couldn't stand rock 'n' roll and thought Elvis's music was "trash." He found Beethoven more inspirational, and wrote that the composer's Fifth Symphony "is the flawless expression of God's Love of triumphant hope and faith and goodness."

One night, the group stayed up and listened to all nine of Beethoven's symphonies.

They often went to the movies or high school sports events in the "Felchmobile"—the convertible coupe owned by his friend Gene Felch—but they were just as likely to gather at someone's house to banter about their ideas for solving the world's problems. President Dwight Eisenhower announced that he would seek reelection in 1956, proud that he had brought about an end to the Korean War and encouraged civil rights legislation in the United States. "There must be no second class citizens in this country," Eisenhower declared.

Jonathan chats with his girlfriend Carolyn Pierce during his junior year in high school. Also shown are classmates Dale Delancy (left) and Gary Howard.

Jonathan was also troubled by inequality, and he refused to sing the last line of "The Star-Spangled Banner": *the land of the free and the home of the brave.* He knew that not everyone was truly free, and he wondered how he would mesh his own desires for his life with the expectations of his parents and society. "Jon was interested in the church from the time I first met him," said Gene Felch. "He liked the role of the minister in the community." Felch believed that Jonathan saw similarities in that role to Dr. Phil Daniels making late-night house calls and treating everyone in need.

Jonathan balanced his seriousness with pranks. One day he and a friend put tacks on a teacher's chair and waited for him to scream. The joke backfired. The teacher sat there for the entire class, never letting on that he was in pain. But he knew who'd done it. As class ended, he called the boys to his desk. "You can have the pleasure of sitting on those same tacks two minutes each or detention," the teacher said.

Jonathan claimed that he'd acted alone, letting his friend off the hook. Jonathan sat on the tacks.

Music proved less painful, but practicing bored him. "He was very unpopular with his music teachers . . . as well as with many of his high school teachers," said Jonathan's mother. "Because he wouldn't work at it." She worried that "he was girl crazy, resentful of all rules, and wrapped up in every activity the school had except classroom work." But Jonathan could pick up nearly any instrument and quickly learn to play it. In the school band, he played the clarinet and the tuba.

Running from band rehearsals to yearbook staff meetings and choir practices kept Jonathan too busy for studying.

Jonathan performs a scene with Keene High School Drama Club president Bonnie Price in this 1957 yearbook photo.

Jonathan had sung with the youth choir at the Congregational church since age seven and gained a reputation as a fine tenor soloist. Choir practice started at 4 p.m. sharp, but one day he rushed into the rehearsal room and said, "I have three places I'm supposed to be right now!" In addition to the choir session, he was due at a drama club rehearsal and high school band practice. The choir director excused him, and he ran off to the high school "to make his peace."

"A TERRIFIC THUD"

Jonathan loved the Congregational choir, but he didn't like the arrogant minister. He also wanted to attend a church with more elaborate ceremonies. But defecting from the Congregationalists would cause trouble in his family, so he kept his mouth shut about it for as long as he could stand it.

He caused his family a different kind of trouble one November night during his junior year. The insurance policy on a friend's new car would take effect at midnight, so they figured, why wait until morning? Jonathan would never be let out of the house that late, especially to go for a joyride with someone his mother didn't approve of.

As midnight approached, the friend leaned a ladder against the house. Jonathan crawled out a bathroom window, made his way across the roof, and climbed down. After a couple of hours of riding around in the car, he hurried back up the ladder.

The night was cold and damp, and frosty moss coated the slanting roof. Jonathan skidded across the shingles and plunged to the frozen ground, landing "with a terrific thud."

**FALLS FROM
ROOF
3,574 DAYS LEFT**

Writhing in pain, Jonathan wasn't about to let his parents
know what he'd done. Somehow he climbed the ladder again
and hobbled to his bedroom. He called his sister for help.

Eventually, Dr. Daniels heard "very odd sounds" coming
from Jonathan's room. He found his son "in awful agony. . . .
What wasn't broken was sprained, bruised, strained,
pulled." His broken ribs made him groan with every breath.

The Daniels home on Summer Street in Keene. Jonathan slipped
off the back roof one night and spent nearly a month in the hospital.

JONATHAN MYRICK
DANIELS
Jon

Home Room Representative
2; JV Cross Country 1;
Second Place (State) American Legion Auxiliary Essay
Contest, First Place 2; Dramatic Club 1, 2, Vice President 3; SALMAGUNDI 2,
Assistant Editor 3; *Enterprise* 1, 2, Associate Editor
3; Band 1, 2, 3; "A" Choir
1, 2, 3; Hi-Y 3; Junior
Rotarian 3.

Band, choir, even cross-country running—Jonathan kept busy
in high school.

Jonathan spent nearly a month in the hospital. It helped that a constant stream of friends came by, violating the hospital's two-visitors-at-a-time rule as they laughed and practiced songs for the school's Christmas concert.

But the hospital stay included long stretches alone, giving Jonathan time to reflect on his poor grades and his sneaky behavior. He didn't like what he saw. "When dawn finally arrived, belatedly, I found myself a trifle behind the eight ball," he wrote. It was time to stop slacking off.

"That really was the turning point, because he did buckle down," his mother said. "I don't mean that he never fooled again or that he spent all his time studying—he certainly didn't—but he did begin to work."

With his schoolwork improving, Jonathan turned to his other big concern: ending his lifelong affiliation with the plain, dry Congregational church and its "know-it-all" minister. That would cause an uproar, but it was a step he felt certain he had to take.

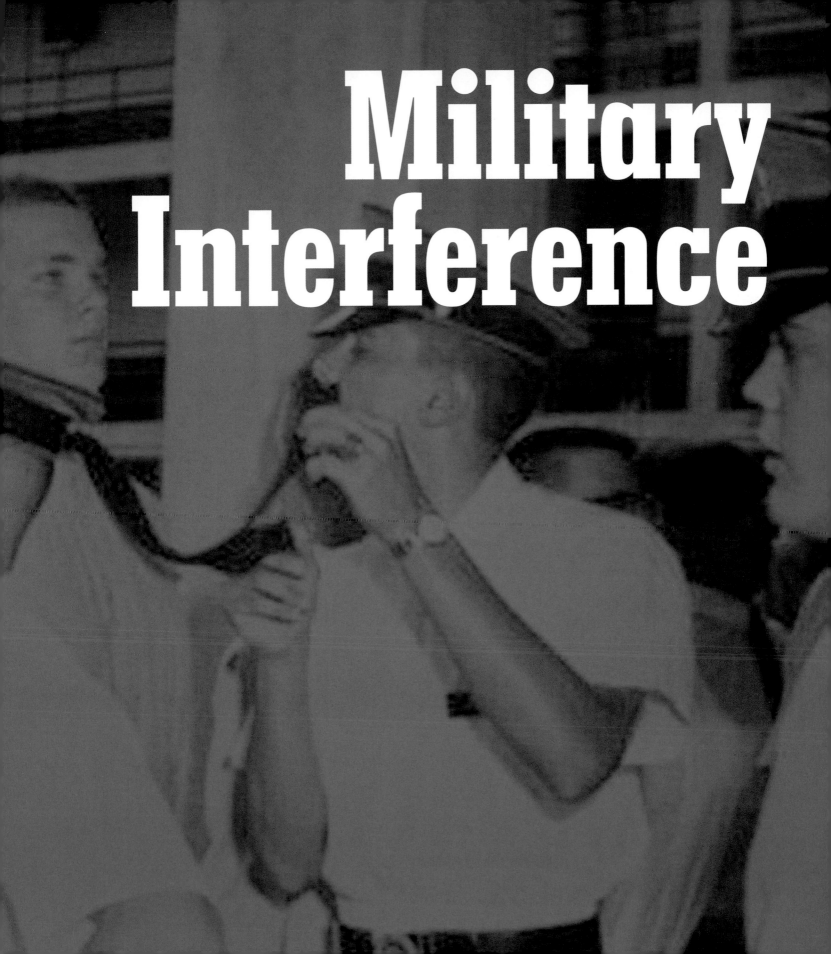

Military
Interference

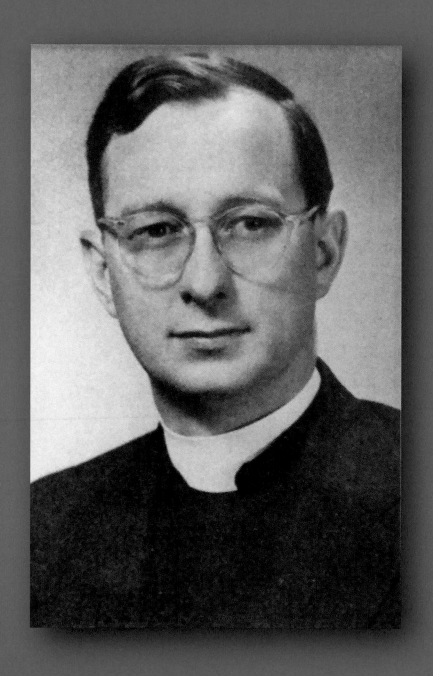

What **Jonathan admired** most about Reverend J. Edison Pike was that the Episcopal priest admitted he didn't have the solutions to life's biggest uncertainties. Jonathan had questions about faith and spirituality, and he knew they couldn't be boiled down to easy explanations. So did Reverend Pike.

"I knew enough to be able to commit my life to what it was and believe in it," Pike said, "but I didn't know all the answers." The priest at Keene's St. James Episcopal Church was a close friend and deer-hunting partner of Dr. Daniels's. His energetic discussions with Jonathan provided exactly the "answers" Jonathan needed as he took a second look at religion and questioned his place in the Congregational church.

Reverend Pike "helped me immeasurably in developing my faith," Jonathan said. During his junior year of high school, he told the priest he wanted to convert to the Episcopal church.

Pike's response surprised him. "I'm not going to accept you into the church." Knowing that Jonathan's defection would set off "an explosion" in the community, he urged him to stay put.

"The whole town would buzz about this," Pike said. Breaking away from the church where he'd spent nearly every Sunday of his life would be too rebellious for Jonathan's parents.

Jonathan cut his ties with the First Congregational Church (left) to join St. James Episcopal Church (right) during his senior year of high school.

Jonathan wouldn't be swayed. Before finishing high school in 1957, he was confirmed at St. James. The rest of his family remained in the First Congregational Church.

An even more surprising change was on the way. Jonathan applied to top colleges like Harvard and Yale, but his grades weren't good enough for him to be accepted. Instead, he made the bewildering decision to attend the Virginia Military Institute (VMI) near that state's Blue Ridge Mountains.

His friends were shocked. Almost nothing about Jonathan suggested that he'd fit in as a cadet at VMI, where students lived in spare barracks, marched daily in military formation on the drill field, did countless push-ups, and followed a strict code of honor. All of the cadets were male.

But Jonathan's family had a long history of military service. In 1942, Jonathan's father had stepped aside from his Keene medical practice to volunteer in the US Army medical corps during World War II. Crawling through a muddy battlefield in Germany to administer morphine to dying soldiers, Dr. Daniels was struck by enemy fire. His feet and legs were injured, and he was awarded a Bronze Star and a Purple Heart. Despite his wounds, he returned to Keene and worked long hours at his medical clinic and the local hospital.

Jonathan's ancestors fought in battles as far back as the Revolutionary War. He wrote that his veins flowed with the blood of "a lieutenant in the Continental Army and a boy (my great-grandfather) who ran away from home to join, after lying about his age, the Union Army as a drummerboy in the Civil War." That last story wasn't quite accurate. Jonathan's great-grandfather George Weaver joined the New Hampshire infantry at age nineteen. His regiment fought in the 1863 Battle of Fort Wagner with the famous Massachusetts

Fifty-Fourth—an all-black regiment—where he earned a medal for bravery.

VMI's cadets fought for the other side during the Civil War, and the Confederate battle flag still flew during Jonathan's time at the school. To most northerners, the flag symbolized racism and slavery.

But Jonathan felt a strong connection to the South. As a young boy, he'd spent time in Kentucky and Arkansas while his father trained for his World War II service. "I think of the South as my adopted home," he wrote in his application to VMI. "I have a great affection, I hope not too disloyal to my country and heritage, for the gallant and valorous but misguided Johnny Rebs"—the nickname for Confederate soldiers.

Jonathan also believed that he'd been too much of a screw-up as a kid, and that he needed more self-discipline. VMI's order and regimentation would force that on him.

A RAT RACE

In 1957, VMI's "Rat" system meant brutal treatment for first-year students like Jonathan. Officers and upperclassmen constantly yelled in the Rats' faces, and physical training was grueling. The worst part was "bracing"—standing in a rigid, uncomfortable posture for hours. The idea was to break a cadet down and then build him up into a soldier.

Jonathan had no intention of becoming a soldier. It didn't take long before he hated VMI. Because of "all the abuse from upperclassmen, and too much studying to be done in too little time—in short, a perpetual rat race—the life of a Rat is somewhat less than ethereal bliss," he wrote to a friend. "One of my Brother Rats has committed suicide—at home—and many have quit."

In this 1961 photo, incoming "Rats" are initiated by VMI upperclassmen. First-year students were ordered to stand in a rigid posture called "bracing."

VMI

Hi Gene:

Thanks for the great letter, old man. I apologize for not having written you sooner, but - as you may imagine - my time is being quite thoroughly occupied. I'm awfully glad that you like Villanova as much as you do. I know you'll do well there, too. I wish I could feel the same way about this place, but I'm afraid that I'm a bit less enthused. This is pure, unadulterated hell, Gene. One of my Brother Rats has committed suicide - at home - and many have quit, two of whom have not gone home. What with "bracing" (a rigid and painful position of attention) and the abuse from upperclassmen, and too

Though nearly six feet tall, Jonathan was so thin that his fellow cadets figured he'd be one of the many new recruits who couldn't tough it out at VMI for even one semester. They didn't like him much. "At first he assumed a distant, if not hostile, attitude toward the southern student," his roommate said, "and took great pride, bordering on the snobbish, in being a member of the Yankee minority."

Jonathan tolerated being "beaten with paddles and coat-hangers at the pleasure of upperclassmen," but he refused to agree with the unjust Rat system.

VMI also brought Jonathan face-to-face with racism. Lexington, Virginia—where the school is located—was strictly segregated, and VMI had no black students. Dormitories faced a courtyard lined with stone decks, or "stoops." The few black workers on campus cleaned that area and ran errands for some cadets. They were called "stoop niggers." That poor treatment caused Jonathan to recognize the racial prejudice in his life and in the town where he was raised. Back in Keene during a school break, he and Gene Felch examined their own biases. For example, an African American named George Miller ran a popular movie theater in Keene. Miller was well liked and respected, but the young men looked back at their relationship with unease. "He called us Mr. Felch and Mr. Daniels and we called him George," Felch said. "We probably would have called him Mr. Miller if he'd been white." And Miller would have called them Gene and Jon.

Jonathan's first lesson in race relations happened much earlier. Like Jonathan's father, another Keene doctor—Albert C. Johnston—applied to serve the country in World War II. Dr. Johnston was African American, and years earlier he'd been denied hospital internships because of his race. Johnston had light skin, so he began to pass as white. When he revealed his true race to the navy, his commission was denied.

After Dr. Johnston was forced to tell the truth, most residents of Keene didn't care, including his friend Dr. Daniels, who worked in the hospital with him. But a 1949 Hollywood movie based on Dr. Johnston's life told a different story. It showed a bigoted response toward the doctor and his family.

Albert and Thyra Johnston gathered their four children for this family portrait in their Keene living room.

The 1949 movie *Lost Boundaries* was based on the life of Keene doctor Albert C. Johnston, who worked in the same hospital as Dr. Daniels. Johnston was African American but chose to pass as white. The critically acclaimed film put Jonathan's hometown in the national spotlight and generated discussion about race relations.

THE TRUE STORY OF A FAMILY WHO LIVED A LIE FOR TWENTY YEARS!

LOUIS DE ROCHEMONT's
"LOST BOUNDARIES"
MEL FERRER
BEATRICE PEARSON

Under the direction of ALFRED L. WERKER
Based on WILLIAM L. WHITE'S document of a New England family
Screen adaptation by Charles Palmer · Screenplay by Virginia Shaler and Eugene Ling

A DRAMA OF REAL LIFE FROM "THE READER'S DIG

The film didn't match Jonathan's experiences with the Johnstons. He and Emily had been guests in the Johnstons' home, and the families sat near each other on Sundays in the Congregational church.

SEEKING JUSTICE

At VMI, Jonathan needed to work harder than ever in the classroom or face failure. He despised the school's "military interference" in every aspect of cadets' lives—particularly in the privacy of their dorm rooms—and he began to speak out against the strict regulations.

Jonathan's room was expected to be precisely the same as every other cadet's, with no personality or signs of individuality. He wasn't even allowed to have a cross on his desk, which bothered him because of his strong religious faith. Unwilling to make that compromise, Jonathan wrote to Reverend Pike for advice.

Pike mailed him a flat, glow-in-the-dark cross about four inches tall. Jonathan thought about where to put it so it wouldn't be detected during daytime inspections. He raised his eyes to the ceiling, slowly chewing a stick of gum until he had an idea.

Four small wads of gum went in the corners of the cross, and Jonathan put a larger one on the end of a broom handle. He stuck the cross to the handle and lifted it to the ceiling, pressing hard until it was firmly in place. The cross was nearly invisible in daylight, but it glowed with the lights off as he gazed up in the dark.

That solved one problem, but Jonathan believed VMI was enforcing religious discrimination. In a letter published in the school's newspaper, he wrote that a cadet should be able to practice his faith just as anyone else could. Since a soldier could be asked to fight for religious freedom, Jonathan wrote, "How can he be expected to defend with his life that which he has not?"

Jonathan continued to speak out for justice. As an upperclassman, he fought against the Rat system and refused to harass the younger cadets. He and the few other upperclassmen who worked to make things better for the first-year students became known as "Rat Daddies." One of the Rats said Jonathan "commanded respect, just in his quiet, contemplative, thoughtful way of conducting himself."

By always speaking his mind, Jonathan gained the respect of his classmates, too. "His words were strong," remarked one cadet, who admired how Jonathan listened to others' ideas and weighed their value. "There was nothing frail about his ideas, nor—even more—about his willingness to admit his error if it were shown him in a clear debate."

Jonathan's professors considered him brilliant, particularly as a writer. "He could talk to professors in their own language, which is not to say he was a stuffy sort of person," recalled a teacher, who said Jonathan was one of the best students he had in his entire career.

Jonathan joined the VMI glee club and the fencing team. He became an editor of the school's newspaper and encouraged other cadets to speak out as he did.

During Jonathan's third year at VMI, Dr. Daniels's World War II injuries began to take a toll. His kidneys were failing. Eventually he needed a wheelchair. Emily was still in high school, so she helped her mother take care of him after school.

Dr. Daniels died two days after Christmas in 1959. He was only fifty-five, and his death was slow and painful. That raised doubts in Jonathan about his faith. Why should such a kind, caring man die so young and in so much pain? Where was the justice in that? Jonathan stopped attending church and seriously questioned his beliefs.

In tribute to his father, Jonathan reconsidered a career in medicine. In addition to his English studies, he doubled up with biology and chemistry courses with an eye toward going to medical school.

AN UPROOTED WEED

Though he never quite fit in at VMI, Jonathan was admired for maintaining his independence and sense of himself in an environment where those traits were usually hammered out of a cadet.

At most schools, the honor of valedictorian is earned by having the highest grades. VMI's valedictorian was elected by the graduating class. Jonathan's classmates found him honest and talented, and they honored him with the election. The northerner—who'd gone from disliked as a Rat to revered as a senior—had made a lasting impression at the southern institution.

In his valedictory speech, Jonathan spoke of his hard times at VMI. In his clear high-pitched voice, he called it "a demanding experience which has monopolized our energies in every conceivable situation. Between the classroom and the drill field, we have been stretched in a great many directions."

Jonathan told of his strongly mixed feelings about the school. "In some colleges one may study for four years without ever allowing the environment to intrude upon his

June 11, 1961

**VMI
VALEDICTORY
SPEECH
1,532 DAYS LEFT**

consciousness. For better or worse, this is not the case at VMI. Whether fertile or barren, in this soil we have planted and extended our roots for four years. Not even the weed can welcome the prospect of being uprooted."

Jonathan recalled some things about VMI with fondness, including "the metallic click of polished heels, the bugler's canonical hours. We shall miss the Blue Ridge Mountains and the green of the valley."

He concluded the speech by wishing his classmates "the decency and the nobility of which you are capable" and "the joy of a purposeful life."

Jonathan's own purpose remained in doubt. His excellent grades earned him a prestigious Danforth scholarship to attend graduate school at Harvard in the fall of 1961. But Harvard suited Jonathan even less than VMI, and he spent a miserable year there. He didn't complete several courses, and he believed that many of his classmates and professors were pompous showoffs, "'shedding false light on non-problems.'"

Actually, Jonathan could be a pompous showoff, too, and that shone through in some of his letters to friends and family. The sophisticated words in his letters sounded more like a professor writing a paper than the funny, relaxed conversations he had in person.

But Jonathan's troubles at Harvard were also the result of a long-delayed reaction to his father's death, and he turned to a psychiatrist for help. "I have undergone what has been variously described as an 'identity crisis,' a 'delayed grief' experience, a religious crisis, and a 'work paralysis,'" he wrote. "In a way, I think each is accurate enough." Adding to the stress was concern about his sister, Emily, who had developed mental health problems while Jonathan was away.

Searching for comfort and direction, Jonathan walked into Boston's Episcopal Church of the Advent on Easter Sunday 1962. The Harvard semester was winding down, and Jonathan was distraught. As he listened to the hymns—sung by a large choir and accompanied by an organ, two violins, and several brass instruments—Jonathan felt a strong reconnection to God and the power of faith.

"I felt His not-so-gentle nudge reminding me that I didn't belong in the graduate school where I was studying," he said. Jonathan yearned to do something more purposeful with his life. He knew what he wanted to do: Leave Harvard. Find a way to become an Episcopal priest.

But his family was broke. When Dr. Daniels died, he left his family in debt. All those years of not asking for money from patients who couldn't pay had taken a toll, so Jonathan's mother enrolled in college to earn a certificate to teach French. With Emily's medical bills piling up, Jonathan quit Harvard and took a train back to Keene in search of work.

Quietly Frantic

More than two hundred thousand people attended the March on Washington for Jobs and Freedom on August 28, 1963. It was the largest civil rights event in American history.

Jonathan landed a job at a company that repaired electric motors, but he wasn't a mechanic. He handled paperwork and sent out bills while coping with his "snarling" bosses.

"The job is beginning to eat it pretty thoroughly," he wrote to a friend after a few months.

But being back in Keene had its rewards, including teaching Sunday school to children at St. James Episcopal Church. Jonathan loved working with the kids and felt energized by them. "Each session that I have had with them has been equivalent to a week's supply of iron pills," he wrote.

Jonathan soon found a more interesting job assisting surgeons at the Keene hospital where his father had worked. The "twenty-four-hour job" meant always being on call, just as Dr. Daniels had been.

More importantly, Jonathan applied for admission to the Episcopal Theological School (ETS), where he could train for the priesthood. He hoped to eventually teach religion at a university.

Back in the family's cluttered house with his mother and his sister, Jonathan thought about his past year. He'd felt directionless since leaving VMI, but applying to ETS gave him a clear path.

"I am quick to see a need and anxious to help," he wrote in his application to the school. "Perhaps because of an intense awareness of my own limitations, I am decidedly more inclined to generosity than to aggression." Among his strengths he listed intelligence, sympathy, and an ability to communicate effectively.

Despite his better mood, he still had doubts about his character. He listed his weaknesses as insecurity, perfectionism, procrastination, and too much concern about how others viewed him.

Jonathan was elated when ETS accepted him as a student, but he would have a long wait. His classes wouldn't begin until the fall of 1963—nearly a year away.

He made the best of his odd year in Keene, blasting classical music, cooking elaborate meals, and dating a much older woman. Now that he was earning money, he prepared feasts of lobster, duckling with orange sauce, or roast lamb with slivers of garlic—leaving the kitchen strewn with dishes. Jonathan put a lot of passion into things that he found important, but he didn't always leave time for cleaning up.

STRIDING TO FREEDOM

Before the start of classes at the seminary, Jonathan joined more than two hundred thousand people at the August 28, 1963, March on Washington. He stood near the front of the crowd, listening intently as the civil rights leader Reverend Dr. Martin Luther King Jr. gave his famous "I Have a Dream" speech at the Lincoln Memorial.

Though Jonathan was an avid writer of letters, he never told anyone that he'd attended the march. There may have been a good reason for that. A photo taken at the march shows Jonathan wearing a priest's collar, and he wouldn't have been eligible to do that. But he was about to enter a seminary, and, like King, he believed that the church should be active in promoting social change. But why would he wear the collar? Perhaps Jonathan believed that white clergy needed to be visible in supporting civil rights, but he wasn't confident that enough would show up for the march. Regardless of why he made the choice, the Episcopal Theological School would not have approved.

Jonathan admired King's activism as a minister and he valued his nonviolent approach in working for civil rights. He'd read King's book *Stride Toward Freedom* and was inspired by King's efforts to bring an end to segregation through peaceful means.

Jonathan listens intently as Reverend Martin Luther King Jr. speaks during the March on Washington. Because Jonathan is wearing a priest's collar, this photo has caused controversy. (See "The Ears Have It" on page 320 to learn how a forensics expert determined that this is Jonathan.)

In his Washington speech, King reminded the throng of marchers that President Abraham Lincoln had signed the Emancipation Proclamation a century earlier, freeing all slaves in any state that had seceded from the Union. But King declared that African Americans were still weighed down by segregation and poverty. The speech was televised, and millions of Americans saw King for the first time.

Spurred on by the speech, Jonathan joined the National Association for the Advancement of Colored People (NAACP). It was an unusual move for a white person, but he was inspired by King.

Jonathan joined the NAACP soon after the March on Washington. He kept the membership card in his wallet.

NAACP 1963

Mr. Jonathan M. Daniels
14 Lawrence Hall
Box 136 ETS
Cambridge 38, Mass.
MEMBER
$3.50
Expires: OCT 1964

UNITED
WE SHALL OVERCOME

READY TO GO

The doubts Jonathan expressed about his own character in his ETS application actually made him better prepared to excel in the school. They revealed a deep self-understanding that few of the other new seminarians had reached. "He came seemingly committed, ready to go, with a background in theology," said a classmate.

The school, which is next to Harvard University in Cambridge, Massachusetts, had only about 125 students—nearly all of them white males, although there were some women and a few black men.

Jonathan had finally found a school that fit his goals and interests. He was learning concepts that he could apply to social issues that were gripping the nation. Motivated by King's speech, he read the works of other theological leaders who advocated nonviolence. He loved to share what he learned with others. At times "he hit on something when he was reading that he'd get excited about," a student in his dorm recalled, "and if you were the next guy to run into him he'd read it to you."

All of the seminarians did fieldwork in the community, which typically meant teaching Sunday school in suburban churches. Jonathan and his roommate Harvel Sanders drew a much tougher assignment. They'd board a train every Saturday for Providence, the capital of Rhode Island, and spend the weekends in a poor urban neighborhood.

Jonathan had developed a habit of never being on time for anything. He kept Sanders waiting the first Saturday, and they sprinted to the station. Alarmed as the train pulled away on its 10:10 a.m. departure, Jonathan raced along the tracks, with Sanders hurrying to keep up. Out of breath, they gave up and waited for the next train. (They always arrived at 10:09 after that.)

The railroad company was bankrupt, and the train to Providence was ancient. Jonathan tried to enjoy the view as the train rocked along the tracks, but rainwater sloshed back and forth between the double panes of the window for the entire trip.

The hour-long train ride provided a perfect introduction to Providence, which also looked run-down. The train stopped near the state house, and Jonathan noticed empty buildings and homes in disrepair as they made their way to Christ Church, where they'd be based.

Sanders said he felt stuck in a time warp. Providence "looked to me like it had never come out of the Depression."

Christ Church once had a large, thriving congregation, but by 1963 most of the white parishioners had left the city. Jonathan stepped into the barnlike old Victorian sanctuary that first Sunday to find it nearly empty. Instead of the several hundred people who once filled the church for services, there were fewer than twenty in attendance.

The neighborhood had been a working-class area of white residents, but the few white people who were left were very poor. Most of the people Jonathan saw that first weekend were black, Portuguese, or mixed race.

Jonathan and Sanders hoped to make the church meaningful for the neighborhood again. They began running a Saturday program for local children that included art lessons and field trips. Little by little Jonathan encouraged the kids to attend Sunday school classes, too. He visited the children's homes, trying to get to know the parents.

Jonathan crams in some studying during his weekend fieldwork in Providence, Rhode Island.

Jonathan tutors a child in Providence.

Jonathan cared deeply for the kids, and he saw the troubles that poverty and a neglected school system could bring. He helped them improve their reading and arithmetic, and he organized games that taught teamwork. He found the work "challenging, tiring, often discouraging," but he also felt uplifted by the progress he made.

On Sunday mornings, the children clashed with "the remnant of the congregation"—the small number of white people who drove in from the wealthier suburbs for church services. That group didn't like how their church was being used by neighborhood kids in the Saturday program. They resented that "street language" from the noisy Sunday school spilled into the nearly empty church during services.

Sanders recalled that the few remaining parishioners felt that "the old world had died and they didn't like what it was being replaced with."

Working closely with the children shifted Jonathan's perspective about what kind of minister he wanted to become. "The program is invaluable to *me*—experientially, ethically, spiritually," he wrote in an evaluation for ETS. "I believe, specifically, that I could serve my Lord with a glad heart in a slum."

On Saturday evenings in Providence, Jonathan and Sanders talked late into the night with the people in charge of the church's urban outreach program. Motivated by the civil rights efforts that Martin Luther King and others were leading in the South, Jonathan spoke of the need for similar work close to home. "You really didn't have much going on in terms of civil rights in Providence," recalled a priest.

Segregation was outlawed in the North, but that didn't mean it didn't exist. The departure of white people from

A staunch opponent of integration, Alabama governor George Wallace was considered by the civil rights movement in the 1960s as the face of resistance.

urban neighborhoods—like downtown Providence—helped bring about de facto segregation in areas where minorities were clustered. In nearby Boston, three thousand black high school students had participated in a one-day boycott of their schools called the Stay Out for Freedom campaign. They were protesting de facto segregation, which kept the mostly black public schools underfunded and poorly maintained.

King called racial segregation evil, whether it was the de facto segregation in the North or legalized segregation in the South, where true segregation was still a way of life. In Alabama, Governor George Wallace did all he could to keep public schools from being integrated, declaring, "Segregation now, segregation tomorrow, segregation forever!"

RISING TENSIONS

During the autumn of 1963, Jonathan became increasingly aware of racial turmoil throughout the country. Just across the Charles River from ETS, black residents of Boston demonstrated for better housing and schools and against violent treatment by police. In Jackson, Mississippi, NAACP activist Medgar Evers had recently been murdered outside his home. And in Birmingham, Alabama, four young black girls were killed when a bomb set by segregationists exploded at the Sixteenth Street Baptist Church. King hurried to Birmingham to lead a nonviolent protest of the bombing and other recent acts of hatred. President John F. Kennedy sent FBI agents and explosives experts to investigate the bombing.

Kennedy advocated civil rights, and he pushed for increased federal funding for education and health care. Two years earlier, Jonathan had marched proudly with his fellow VMI cadets at Kennedy's inaugural parade. The new president's inspiring speech fit perfectly with Jonathan's belief that "self-fulfillment lies in service," which he'd learned from his father. Kennedy spurred the crowd to action with his inaugural address. "In the long history of the world, only a few generations have been granted the role of defending freedom in its hour of maximum danger," he said. "I do not shrink from this responsibility—I welcome it. . . . And so, my fellow Americans: ask not what your country can do for you—ask what you can do for your country."

Kennedy stood for many of the ideals Jonathan cared about. "We were somehow riding the crest of a wave of reform and change," one seminarian explained. "Wonderful things were going to happen, not because of us, but we were a part of it."

But Jonathan and his classmates underestimated how strongly others would fight against progress. In November 1963, that resistance took another violent turn when Kennedy was assassinated in Dallas, Texas.

"All of a sudden it seemed as if everything was changed," a classmate said. "When Kennedy was shot, we didn't know what to make of it. It just sobered us up."

Vice President Lyndon B. Johnson became president, and he urged the US Congress to pass a civil rights bill as a tribute to Kennedy. The bill would prohibit segregation in public places throughout the country and ban employment discrimination on the basis of race, color, religion, gender, or national origin.

Jonathan marched with his fellow VMI cadets past the presidential reviewing stand during the inaugural parade for President John F. Kennedy on January 20, 1961.

NEW TACTICS

President Johnson signed the civil rights bill into law in the summer of 1964, just as Jonathan began a twelve-week program that thrust him even further from the boundaries of his experience. He was assigned to the Willard Psychiatric Institute in upstate New York to work with severely mentally ill adults. He'd be exploring how to counsel troubled people—an important part of a minister's work.

Some patients were locked in padded rooms to keep them from hurting themselves. They "screamed and yelled and hollered and swore and all that stuff all day long," said the priest who supervised Jonathan and five other seminarians at Willard.

Jonathan's assignment involved visiting patients, alone, in their rooms, and interviewing them about their lives. "You're walking dead cold on the wards, scared to death," said the supervisor. "Here are these people with serious problems . . . and there you are. All you've got is yourself."

Jonathan was accustomed to winning people over with his intelligence and sense of humor, but he found the patients unpredictable. His usual tactics didn't work, so he began to rely on his ability to listen. He spent much of his time with the younger patients, particularly a woman who had frequent epileptic seizures. Staff members believed that she faked the seizures—not an easy thing to do. They ignored her or yelled at her to stop.

The woman had been a patient at Willard for several years and no one had made any progress toward helping her. But Jonathan saw similarities between her attitude and his own; he never liked being told how to act either. He spent much of the summer talking to the woman, and more importantly, listening to her as she spoke about her life and her frustrations. At first she resisted his help, but Jonathan eventually convinced her that talking about her problems was better than faking seizures. The seizures stopped completely.

Jonathan had discovered that a trait he'd viewed as one of his weaknesses could actually become an advantage: questioning a person's motives. By catching someone off guard, he could cause them to take a hard inward look and make a change.

NO EXCUSES

When he returned to ETS in the fall of 1964, Jonathan and the other seminarians crowded into the TV room. The newscasts were "filled with civil rights stuff," recalled one classmate. Jonathan continued to spend weekends in Providence, where the outreach program thrived. He encouraged neighborhood teenagers to attend Saturday evening drop-in events, which became so popular the floor sagged under the weight of the participants.

Jonathan was making a difference, and he was overjoyed that the teenagers began to trust him. "It is so great to watch a hostile kid begin to love," he wrote. "Some cases I can only regard as quiet miracles—they just aren't the same kids anymore."

With his heavy schedule of classes and a new part-time job managing the ETS bookstore, Jonathan described his life as "quietly frantic." But he continued to earn high grades and praise from his professors. "I couldn't ask [for] a more perfect semester," he wrote during a short winter break. He was thrilled about his upcoming courses, including "Sin and

Forgiveness in the New Testament," "Christian Ethics," and "Marriage and Family Counseling."

Jonathan was eager to make another positive change, too: cleaning up his living quarters. "My rooms resemble a pigsty at the moment—papers, books, exam booklets, unanswered bills and letters, clothes, you name it *everywhere*." Despite the clutter, he was finally happy and confident.

Jonathan had become friends with one of the few female seminarians, a spirited twenty-two-year-old Radcliffe College graduate from St. Louis named Judy Upham. "I'd seen him kind of off and on without noticing him particularly except as a nice guy and lots of fun to talk to," she said. Stressed from an overload of classwork one day, they had lunch together.

"He was in a foul mood and I was in a foul mood, and we spent the whole time growling at each other so we would have someone to growl at who wouldn't complain," Judy said. "We both went away in much better humor."

Getting together regularly for lunch or dinner, they talked about music and movies and their plans for the future. Jonathan mentioned that he needed to paint his newly straightened rooms.

"Gee, I love to paint," Judy replied. She brushed the walls brown while Sanders and Jonathan painted the trim and fireplace "a very elegant" white and black. Then they celebrated by going to see an opera film.

Judy enjoyed Jonathan's sarcastic sense of humor, and he impressed her with his manners. "He always held doors for people, and would help you on with your coat."

During a long walk beside the Charles River one very cold evening, Judy and Jonathan talked about the meaning of life. As snow swirled around them, Jonathan explained that he didn't care about money or status, but he felt certain that social activism would play a prominent role in whatever path he took.

Jonathan had no intention of playing it safe by staying in the background; he'd seen too many seminarians and ministers who preferred to pray for progress rather than take an active role. "I have an uncomfortable feeling that one of my lingering temptations is going to be to try to play at being God rather than enduring the risk of being a man," he wrote to a friend. "And that is both blasphemy and a lousy excuse for healthy human experience."

Interest in racial injustice became much sharper at ETS in early 1965 after news arrived from Alabama. The seminarians learned that the state's Episcopal bishop had barred civil rights workers from the church. Bishop Charles C. J. Carpenter staunchly supported segregation, and he criticized Episcopalians who participated in efforts to promote equal rights for blacks.

Jonathan was "bitterly opposed to racial prejudice" and believed segregation was morally wrong, but he felt he couldn't do anything about Carpenter's order. Jonathan's opinion quickly changed when Alabama erupted in racial violence. He wouldn't sit still and pray while that happened.

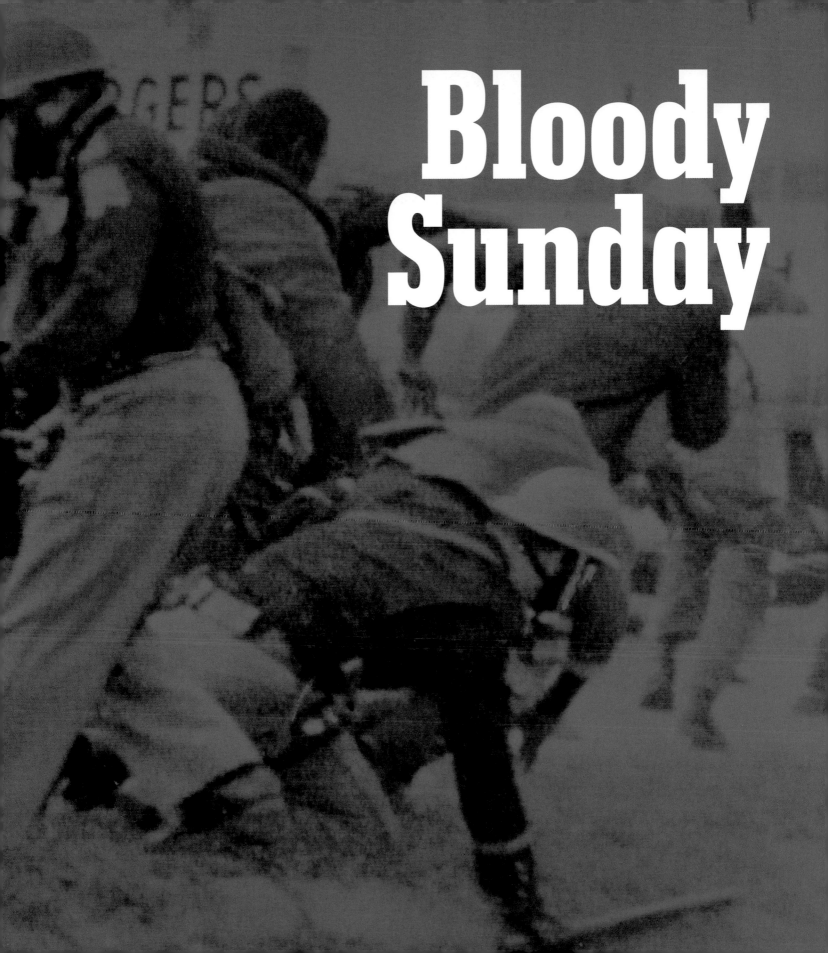

Bloody Sunday

The only things Selma, Alabama, and Cambridge, Massachusetts, had in common on the Sunday afternoon of March 7, 1965, were bone-chilling temperatures. As Jonathan stepped off the train from Providence and braced for the cold walk to his newly painted dorm room, twenty-five-year-old civil rights leader John Lewis faced the biting Selma wind head on. The same age as Jonathan, Lewis also dreamed of becoming a minister. As a child, he'd preached to the chickens on his family's Alabama farm while Jonathan gave sermons in the Skull and Bones space below his New Hampshire home.

Now Lewis led a line of six hundred black protesters headed across the Alabama River to see Governor George Wallace. They were angry that a white state trooper had killed Jimmie Lee Jackson, an unarmed black man, at a peaceful voting rights march and got away with it. They were determined to walk fifty-four miles to the state capitol in Montgomery to protest police brutality and demand equal voting rights.

Stuffed in their coat pockets were toothbrushes in case they were arrested. Lewis expected that he'd be jailed longer, since he was chairman of the civil rights group called the Student Nonviolent Coordinating Committee (SNCC—pronounced *snick*), which had been working in Selma to ensure voting rights. He'd tossed an apple and an orange into

Civil rights leaders John Lewis (right) and Hosea L. Williams lead marchers across the Edmund Pettus Bridge on March 7, 1965. Directly behind them are Bob Mants (right) and Albert Turner. Charles Mauldin is behind Turner.

his knapsack. But no one expected such frigid temperatures or what waited for them on the other side of the river.

Clutching woolen scarves, they crossed the Edmund Pettus Bridge, walking silently, two by two. The men marched at the front and the back of the line to protect the women and children, who held hands in the middle. But as they reached the crest of the bridge over the rushing Alabama River, Lewis spotted a sea of blue uniforms.

One hundred and fifty Alabama state troopers stood shoulder to shoulder, blocking the other side. Dallas County sheriff Jim Clark waited with his nightstick, too, a weapon well known to the marchers. Clark's posse of special deputies rode on horseback, carrying bullwhips and barely keeping their mounts from charging.

Lewis and the group kept walking. Then came the order: "This demonstration will not continue!" an officer shouted into a bullhorn. "I will give you two minutes to leave!"

Lewis needed to act swiftly. "Can you swim?" a marcher asked him. It was a long way down to the river. "No," Lewis replied. Suddenly, he knew what to tell the marchers.

Huddled in the TV room at ETS, Jonathan was in a heated discussion about the Vietnam War, where the United States backed South Vietnam in its battles against North Vietnam's communist regime. Though he wouldn't be drafted because of his asthma, Jonathan made it clear that he'd be willing to go to jail instead of to war. He was still angry about President Johnson's announcement earlier in the week. Johnson had given the go-ahead to bomb North Vietnam. The first American combat troops were on their way.

Alabama state troopers
in gas masks wait
on the far side of the
Edmund Pettus Bridge.
Officers bludgeoned
and tear-gassed
the marchers moments
later in an attack
that became known as
Bloody Sunday.

Jonathan didn't pay much attention to a television program about Nazis blaring in the background until a breaking news story interrupted the show. Expecting it to be about Vietnam, someone cranked up the volume. But the news footage was from Selma, Alabama. John Lewis had turned around and told the marchers to kneel down and pray, but he was too late. Troopers had strapped on their gas masks, raised their weapons, and stormed into the crowd.

Jonathan watched in horror as the peaceful marchers who were protesting police brutality became the victims of it. A state trooper clubbed Lewis in the head and he crumpled to the ground. The posse on horseback whipped women and children blinded by clouds of noxious tear gas. But who could outrun a charging stallion?

"The sight of them rolling over us like human tanks was something that had never been seen before," Lewis recalled. Americans watching on TV were outraged and ashamed. They anticipated war footage from Vietnam, half a world away, not bloody battle scenes within their own country.

"I don't understand how President Johnson can send troops to Vietnam," Lewis said before being rushed to the hospital with a fractured skull, "and cannot send troops to Selma, Alabama, to protect people whose only desire is to register to vote." The attack became known as Bloody Sunday.

Nearby, in a Selma motel room, Reverend John Morris was making phone calls after listening helplessly to the police beatings on a radio. Morris—who would soon become Jonathan's mentor—had founded the Episcopal Society for Cultural and Racial Unity (ESCRU) to fight segregation and to pressure the Episcopal Church to embrace change. The white Georgia native telephoned his close friend Martin

John Lewis is brutally beaten by an Alabama state trooper. "My legs fell under me," Lewis said. "I thought I was going to die on that bridge."

Luther King in Atlanta, urging him to lead a march from Selma to Montgomery on Tuesday, this time with the support of sympathetic whites from across the country. Morris knew that King's presence was essential to bring more attention to what the marchers strived to achieve. King had been in Selma several times that year to lead voting rights marches, and he'd been arrested and spent time in jail.

Morris was convinced from his phone calls that he could round up a hundred white clergy for a ministers' march. He helped King compose a telegram.

Believing that ending racism was the responsibility of all religious leaders, Morris suggested that King "call on the clergy of the nation to . . . help *bear this burden*."

King agreed. That night he wired an urgent telegram to churches and seminaries, including ETS. Using Morris's suggestion, King described the brutality against the marchers and insisted that Selma residents would continue to stand for justice. But he also asked that others join them and bear the burden—particularly members of the clergy.

But what exactly did King mean by *bear the burden*?

John Lewis knew. "He wanted to see," Lewis explained, "whether the state troopers, Sheriff Clark, and the local police would use the same force and degree of brutality against these white citizens from the North as they did against poor black folks."

For Jonathan, the talk of Vietnam was over. His focus was now on freedom at home and the black Americans who didn't have it.

WHOSE PROBLEM?

The next morning, King's plea to northern clergy dominated the conversations at ETS. "There was trouble in Selma, as we all knew," Jonathan wrote. But he didn't have enough money for a plane ticket and he didn't own a car that he could drive to Alabama.

As he hurried to grab a coffee before heading to his Monday classes, Jonathan overheard students talking about raising money to attend the Selma ministers' march. They said that a chartered plane would leave Boston for Atlanta at nine o'clock that night.

Excited by the news, Jonathan hoped to be onboard. "I raced back to Lawrence Hall, flew up the three flights, and hurled myself into the room of a friend," he said. Shaking the friend awake, Jonathan couldn't convince him to go. What had sounded like a good idea the night before now seemed impractical. *Too busy* was a common reaction from other students. *It isn't our problem.*

Jonathan's roommate, Harvel Sanders, didn't want to disrupt his school year. "I think that's where many of us were," Sanders explained. "Jon was simply willing to allow his life to be interrupted by this."

Ed Rodman, a black first-year student from Virginia, had a different reason for staying. As a teenager, he'd been active in the civil rights movement, but he had no interest in traveling to Selma. He thought he could make more of a difference closer to ETS. "There was plenty to do in South Boston," Rodman said.

Disappointed, Jonathan rushed to class but couldn't concentrate. *Can I spare the time to go to Selma*, he kept thinking. *Do I want to spare the time?*

"Reluctantly I admitted to myself that the idea was impractical," he said. "I tucked in an envelope my contribution to the proposed 'Selma fund.'"

His friend Judy Upham did the same thing. "I wasn't going. It was a crazy thing," she remembered, even though Selma was becoming "this huge war."

As contributions poured in, Jonathan knelt in the seminary chapel for evening prayers, searching for a sign. Even as he'd stuffed money into an envelope for someone else's trip, he knew he had to be on that plane. All his life he'd found ways to overcome challenges. He'd worked against

"Sometimes the call comes at the least convenient moment you can imagine. But whenever it comes, you must go."

— JONATHAN DANIELS

unfair treatment at VMI and found ways to better people's lives in Providence. Here was a much bigger injustice where he could make a difference. It would be easy to ignore, but could he live with himself if he didn't go to Selma?

Two hours before the plane departed, Jonathan found his answer. It was hidden in the closing words of an evening prayer called the Magnificat that, to him, spoke about equality. "I knew then," he said, "that I must go to Selma."

Jonathan looked for Judy. "Hey! You coming?" he asked.

"Yes, well, I guess so," she replied. They rushed to the airport.

The chartered plane was packed with seminary students and clergy from different faiths, including a bow-tied Unitarian minister named James Reeb. They arrived in Atlanta at three o'clock on Tuesday morning, March 9.

With no place to stay, Jonathan and the other seminarians rode to the headquarters of the Southern Christian Leadership Conference (SCLC). Led by King, the SCLC promoted spiritual principles while working for civil rights in a nonviolent way. The ETS contingent took over King's private office on the first floor and tried to sleep. King was already in Selma and wide awake, working out details for the day's march.

Still in the clothes he'd worn since Boston, Jonathan tried to spread out on the floor. Judy claimed the leather couch. "I never did get to sleep really," Judy said. "Every available inch of floor space was taken up by people in sleeping bags."

By 7 a.m., Jonathan was anxious to hop on a chartered bus for Selma. Everyone lining up for those buses planned to march because of the brutality they'd witnessed on TV. But unlike most of the marchers on Bloody Sunday, Jonathan and the other white northerners had their freedom and they could vote.

WHITE ONLY

Jonathan took this photo at a Selma laundry.

SEGREGATED SOCIETY

Jonathan knew that life in Selma had never been easy for African Americans, but by 1965 voting should have been. Nearly a hundred years before, the Fifteenth Amendment to the US Constitution had guaranteed it. But the amendment

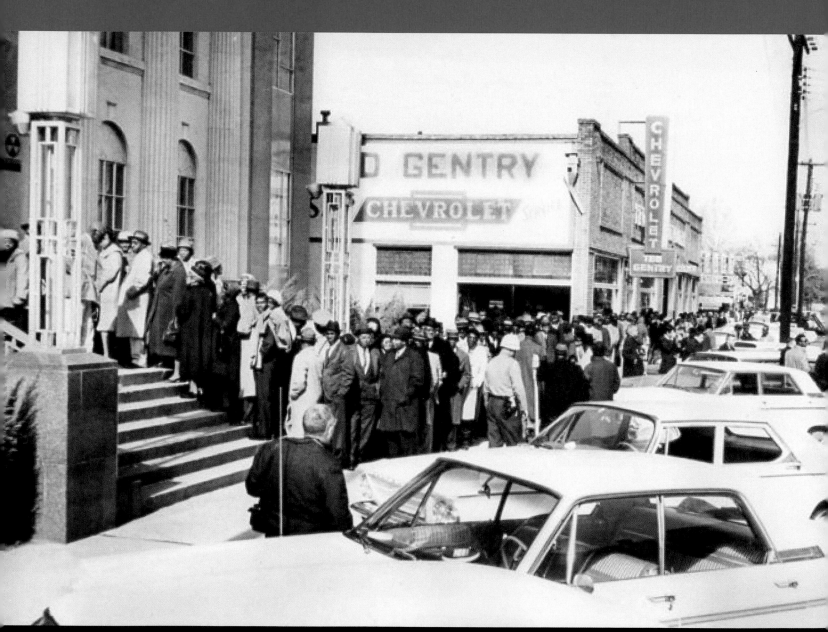

Black men and women form a long line as they wait to register to vote outside the Dallas County Courthouse in Selma.

seemed doomed from the start. First, it excluded women from voting, regardless of their race. Second, southern segregationists were committed to keeping blacks as second-class citizens.

For a short time, black men *did* vote, and two former slaves from Selma were elected to the US Congress in the 1870s. But restrictions began almost immediately. Southern state governments issued voting taxes and "literacy" tests for blacks, which were really trivia quizzes nearly impossible to answer.

Things grew worse in 1896 when the US Supreme Court crushed the constitutional protections of African Americans by agreeing to a "separate but equal society" in the South. Not only did this mean segregation, but it also meant that it was legally acceptable to discriminate against blacks through a set of laws and customs called Jim Crow.

The 1964 Civil Rights Act was supposed to end segregation and Jim Crow, but it wasn't working and it hadn't addressed voting rights. Blacks still couldn't shake hands with whites or eat with them in southern restaurants. If they rode in the same car, blacks had to be in the backseat. And they could never question the character of a white person, even if that person was lying. If they did, they'd be fired from their jobs or worse: beaten, jailed, or killed.

In 1965, only 2 percent of the Selma area's black majority was registered to vote. Adding to the obstacle of those literacy tests was the police brutality led by Dallas County sheriff Jim Clark. Despising blacks who stood up for their rights, the angry sheriff was like a time bomb ready to explode. The six-foot-four Clark arrested or clubbed anyone lined up to register who asked questions.

Dallas County sheriff Jim Clark (center) and his deputies used force to keep blacks from voting.

"Clark was just a mean man," said a woman who witnessed his tactics.

Selma teenagers were tired of the treatment. The voting age was twenty-one, so they were too young to vote. But many skipped school and marched to encourage their parents to register and stand up to Clark. He sent the teens to jail, too, or forced them with electric cattle prods to run for miles until they vomited.

Selma students demonstrate for their parents' voting rights in February 1965.

Students kneel on a
Selma sidewalk in 1965
after being arrested
for protesting.

DO NOT STRIKE BACK

As Jonathan boarded the bus in Atlanta, he could feel the tension. He smiled at the white driver, who glared at him and the other northerners. Ignoring the slight, Jonathan focused on keeping warm, but couldn't help shivering in his seat because of the freezing temperature. He'd expected the south to be mild and had worn only light clothing. It was cold enough to see his breath, so Jonathan and the group sang freedom songs while trying to warm up during the four-hour ride to Selma.

The cold would soon become the least of Jonathan's troubles that morning. Terrified that the bus might be attacked by segregationists, the driver pulled over near Selma. He refused to go any farther, and a new driver had to be called in.

A black teenage civil rights worker also came aboard. She reminded the passengers that the march to Montgomery was to be a peaceful one. "Be prepared to face arrest," she warned before giving instructions on how to participate in nonviolent demonstrations: If struck, do not strike back. Instead, curl into the fetal position and protect the back of your neck and your face with your arms.

Noticing that the women wore skirts, the teen advised them to change into pants, but most had only the clothes they were wearing.

Finally, the streets of Selma came into view, giving Jonathan his first glimpse of the city's racial inequality. Paved streets lined Selma's white sections, and construction crews were widening them. Black neighborhoods had dirt roads of red clay, including the bus's destination—Sylvan Street in front of Brown Chapel.

State troopers and sheriff's officers patrol outside Selma's Brown Chapel after the Bloody Sunday beatings.

With a court order in place forbidding civil rights gatherings, demonstrators relied on churches. Brown Chapel—an African Methodist Episcopal church—became the headquarters for Selma's civil rights movement. The second bus driver was afraid to take them there. Instead, he dropped them off in a field two miles away. Walking into town, Jonathan came face-to-face with how segregationists felt about the northern visitors. Angry whites sitting on their porches heckled the newcomers.

The group reached Brown Chapel, which is surrounded by the red-brick buildings of the George Washington Carver Homes—a federal housing project for black residents. The church was so crowded that Jonathan and Judy couldn't get in. ESCRU's Reverend Morris had hoped a hundred white clergy members would show up, but four hundred preachers, nuns, and rabbis had responded to King's call. Jonathan milled about the property with the newcomers and thousands of local residents. A lawyer thrust an identification form at him, insisting that he sign it in case he was arrested or killed. It was a reminder that the theories of nonviolence Jonathan had been reading about might soon be put into action.

Inside Brown Chapel, King and his advisors finalized plans for the ministers' march—the second attempt to march from Selma to Montgomery. Since January, King had been bringing national attention to Selma's voting rights campaign. And he proved correct in predicting that once the rest of the nation saw Sheriff Clark in action, Americans would rush to right the injustice. But with Governor Wallace promising to block the day's march, negotiations continued, and it would be several hours before anything happened.

Reverend Martin Luther King Jr. preaches in Selma's Brown Chapel. The church became a safe haven for civil rights leaders and the site of frequent mass meetings.

READY TO MARCH

Hurry up and wait became a common theme for the civil rights movement and something Jonathan would have to get used to. While Judy stayed with their gear, he went to buy a candy bar. He was eager, but like most of the marchers he wasn't very well prepared. Jonathan expected to spend several days and nights on the trek to Montgomery, even though he hadn't packed warm clothing or blankets.

King emerged from Brown Chapel and the crowd cheered. Jonathan rushed back from the store and lined up for the march.

With King leading the way, the crowd of two thousand headed down Sylvan Street toward the Edmund Pettus Bridge, where marchers had been beaten two days earlier on Bloody Sunday. They filled the streets for six blocks. Jonathan linked arms with his line and they stayed close together, not knowing what to expect. As the line of marchers stretched out, they took up several different freedom songs.

> *Ain't gonna let nobody turn me 'round*
> *I'm gonna keep on a-walking,*
> *Keep on a-talking,*
> *Marching up to freedom land.*

"Nobody was really keeping in time because there'd be a chunk here singing and a chunk there singing," Judy recalled. "It was really amazing."

The marchers began walking across the bridge, but when they reached the other side, they abruptly stopped. Standing under the bridge's gray arches, Jonathan craned his neck and tried to see what was happening up ahead

King had agreed not to go farther than the end of the bridge, so he knelt down and prayed. He'd made a deal with a judge to honor a restraining order not to march beyond the bridge that day, in hopes of receiving the go-ahead to lead the full march to Montgomery later in the week. But only King's closest advisors knew about the agreement. For the rest of the demonstrators, being turned around without walking any farther than the courageous demonstrators on Bloody Sunday seemed like a failure.

"They only let us walk across the bridge. Well, crud!" Judy said about the halted march, which became known as Turnaround Tuesday. She and Jonathan felt "a little bit double-crossed" about the secret agreement.

Disappointed and ready to go back to ETS, most of the group flew home that night, but Jonathan and Judy stayed. King had encouraged them not to leave yet, certain that approval for the march to Montgomery would happen soon. Jonathan, Judy, and white clergy who remained headed for a meeting at Brown Chapel, which was packed with parishioners.

"Both doors opened and in came the clergy from everywhere—mostly white," recalled Joyce Parrish O'Neal, who was fifteen at the time. "That night was so special after what had happened on Bloody Sunday, the violence. The idea that so many people would risk their lives to come help us. . . . It was very dangerous for white people."

Jonathan was stunned by the welcome they received. Parishioners insisted that he and the other white marchers sit in the front row. "We felt a little embarrassed about it," Judy admitted. "It was their church and their movement, and we were almost kind of butting in."

With his head bandaged from Bloody Sunday, John Lewis disagreed. "It demonstrated a great deal of support to the local people," he said about the help from white northerners. "We needed it."

For most of the more than two hundred black families living in the George Washington Carver Homes, their experiences with whites had been negative. Ku Klux Klansmen frequently drove the streets at night, blasting their horns and shooting at streetlights. Many residents were raised with a warning: stay away from whites. True, the federal housing project had become like a second headquarters for the movement. But so far, very few of the workers were white.

At the Brown Chapel gathering, King asked residents of the Carver Homes to put their fear of whites aside and "help the people get somewhere to stay," a woman recalled. No hotels in Selma would rent rooms to "outside agitators," and sleeping at the homes of whites was out of the question.

Despite the fears, Jonathan and Judy were welcomed into the home of Rosa Scott and her children, whose backyard bordered Brown Chapel.

DEADLY ENCOUNTER

That evening, James Reeb—the bow-tied Unitarian minister from Boston who'd flown on the same plane as Jonathan and Judy—left Brown Chapel to get a bite to eat. Reeb walked with his friends past the Silver Moon Cafe, a notorious meeting spot for the Ku Klux Klan and Sheriff Clark and his posse.

A mob of angry whites outside the cafe attacked the group. One took a swing at Reeb's head with a club like a baseball bat, knocking him unconscious. By the time he reached a hospital, Reeb had slipped into a coma. He died shortly after and became the first white civil rights worker murdered in 1965.

King had his answer. Within forty-eight hours of issuing his plea to northern clergy, he'd learned that Alabama whites *would* kill other whites who helped blacks seek equality. Even if that white person was a minister.

Unitarian minister James Reeb was beaten to death in Selma.

Open Hostility

Prisoners in striped uniforms are ordered to set up barricades, which quickly became known as Selma's "Berlin Wall." The name referred to the wall separating the city of West Berlin in West Germany from Communist East Berlin in East Germany.

The restraining order halting the march from Selma to Montgomery had not yet been lifted. Frustrated by the stalling and angered by the bludgeoning of Reverend Reeb, Jonathan questioned his role in Selma. "At the moment I can't imagine that I have anything to give of any significance," he wrote.

Other demonstrations continued, so Jonathan joined Wednesday's march from Brown Chapel to Selma's Dallas County Courthouse to protest Reeb's beating. As the demonstrators began the nine-block walk to the courthouse, city police halted them. Selma's mayor suddenly declared a state of emergency and banned all marches.

Fearing a repeat of Bloody Sunday, the mayor hoped to contain the city's black residents and the integrated group of protesters, and to protect them from Sheriff Clark. He ordered convicts in striped jail uniforms to haul wooden barricades to the front of Brown Chapel and the roads leading into the Carver Homes. Within minutes, Selma's black neighborhood was blocked off from the rest of the world.

The mayor put Wilson Baker in charge of the blockade. Wearing thick glasses, a suit, and a fedora hat, the cigar-smoking Baker was Selma's public safety director, and he clashed with Sheriff Clark. Baker opposed Clark's violent treatment of blacks, but Baker was still a segregationist.

Jonathan joined a group of angry teenagers from Selma's all-black R. B. Hudson High School, determined to stand by the barriers and demand that the blockades be taken down.

Jonathan (partly obscured to the right of the deputy's helmet) stands defiantly at Selma's Berlin Wall.

He stood face-to-face with police who were ready to crack his skull with a gun or a billy club.

"We are going to stop any demonstrations," Baker announced as he eyed the protesters. "It is too risky under the present circumstances." Part of that risk stood right behind him: Sheriff Clark and his club-wielding posse. Baker controlled law and order in the city, but if the protesters reached the county courthouse, they'd fall prey to Clark.

Some of the wooden barriers collapsed as Jonathan and the other demonstrators pushed forward. Baker replaced them with rope that came to be known as the "Berlin Wall." Police carrying guns and clubs patrolled every section of it.

"The air crackled with tension and frustration and open hostility," Jonathan wrote. Caught behind the wall and the police officers guarding it, he refused to leave or back down. Jonathan didn't like being restrained or pushed around, and he felt the frustration of the black residents, who'd faced that for their entire lives. He wanted to help lead the way.

"We're going to march, we're going to march!" Jonathan and the demonstrators chanted. Intent on walking to the courthouse to protest Reeb's beating and this new oppression by the police, the teenagers made up songs about bringing down the wall.

CURSING AND PRAYING

Heavy rain fell and it continued for days, flooding the dirt streets. Soaking wet, Jonathan assembled tarps for shelter. He and the protesters stayed by the rope day and night. He hoped to make some kind of progress, though he didn't know what that would be. But he could sense that this movement of young black people would bring about great changes. "I have the haunting feeling again and again that I am flying with the mightiest Wind in the world at my back," he wrote.

The high school students waved signs reading WE WILL BE FREE and OH FREEDOM at the menacing officers on horseback who blocked the neighborhood.

At night, Jonathan slept in the muddy streets on blankets hauled out by the students' parents. Tired and hungry, he was grateful for the bologna sandwiches and hot coffee passed along the line.

"Jonathan's presence there was important not just as a white man, but as a white man who was compassionate," said Hattie Austin, who at age fifteen stood with Jonathan at the wall. "He emboldened us to make a difference in our lives," and "he wasn't much older than we were."

Jonathan felt the same way about the teenagers. "In a strange way, this beloved community within the Negro compound have become my people," he wrote, referring to his friends "who ate and slept and cursed and prayed in the rain-soaked streets."

Those friends included nine-year-old Sheyann Webb. She'd escaped the whips and horses' hooves of Sheriff Clark's posse on Bloody Sunday. Now she wondered why a white man like Jonathan, who already had his freedom, fought so hard to break through the wall. "We weren't accustomed to having a relationship with a white person, period," she remembered.

"He would hold our hands when we'd be in the street singing," recalled Sheyann's best friend, Rachel West, who was ten at the time. "He made me feel more secure when he was with me."

That sense of security extended to another student, Emma Jean Greene, a sophomore at Hudson High School. As she and Jonathan spoke, a surge of protesters pushed toward the barriers, and they were separated. "Jonathan, get back here before you get hurt," Emma Jean called.

Caught up in the crowd's defiance, Jonathan wouldn't budge. "My determination had become infectiously savage," he recalled, "and I insisted that she come forward—I would not retreat!" He grabbed the girl's hand and led her to the front of the crowd.

Sheriff Jim Clark's button says NEVER as he patrols the Berlin Wall. Clark fiercely opposed integration, and, true to the word on his button, he never changed his stance.

Tensions run high as police halt demonstrators attempting to march in protest of James Reeb's murder.

A young police officer scowled at him. "You're dragging her through the puddle," he told Jonathan. "You ought to be ashamed for treating a girl like that."

"And whose fault is that?" Jonathan yelled back. The confrontation demanded nonviolence, but he was losing his temper. Jonathan quickly regretted it. It was one thing to study about nonviolence, another to practice it in the face of an angry officer. Jonathan apologized to the officer and asked his name. It was Charlie.

Jonathan and the teenagers started singing, *We love Charlie!* The officer blushed. For a moment the tension melted. "We all lit cigarettes (in a couple of instances, from a common match)," Jonathan wrote, "and small groups of kids and policemen clustered to joke or talk cautiously about the situation."

A NEW CHALLENGE

Anyone wanting to leave the area behind the wall had to request permission from Wilson Baker. Jonathan told Baker that he planned to visit St. Paul's Episcopal Church. He'd been in Selma only for a few days, but he was alarmed that the church was segregated. That didn't fit his ideas of how his church should act, and he intended to change it.

Baker had little sympathy for Jonathan's idea. "I'm not interested in freedom or anything," Baker replied. "I'm interested in protecting the lives of the people in this city." But Jonathan persuaded Baker to let him go.

Jonathan confronted Reverend Frank Mathews, the blond, blue-eyed priest at St. Paul's, about the church's practices. Like everything else in the South, places of worship—at least the ones attended by whites—were segregated. The discriminatory practice went against religious doctrines, but that didn't stop priests, rabbis, and ministers from turning away blacks.

Reverend Mathews believed in segregation. "We are not all made alike," he preached to his congregation.

Mathews's attitude stemmed from the prejudiced belief that whites were superior to blacks. The damaging lie was so popular in 1965 that Martin Luther King kept trying to set the record straight. He reminded audiences that some individuals were smarter than others, but that there was no such thing as a superior race.

Reverend Mathews glared at Jonathan as he stood outside the church. When Jonathan asked what would happen if blacks attended the Sunday service, the jittery priest, who suffered from bleeding ulcers, hesitated. "What would you do if someone with measles tried to come to your church?" he finally replied.

Jonathan reminded Mathews that being black wasn't a contagious disease and that segregation violated the laws of the Episcopal Church. He warned that St. Paul's could be shut down. Mathews insisted that it wasn't up to him, but to the ushers who seated the worshippers.

That Sunday, March 14, Jonathan brought the Scott children with him to St. Paul's. As they approached the wooden doors, the ushers locked arms and refused to let them in. But Jonathan wouldn't leave. He believed it was his duty to protest the church's injustice, so he knelt on the sidewalk and prayed. He "was a rebel of the church," a friend recalled. Jonathan's "own hope was that he would not become a rebel of the church but that the type of work he did would be the type of work that the church would do."

Though refused entry with his black friends, Jonathan wasn't through with St. Paul's. He'd failed in his first attempt to integrate the church, but he vowed to try again.

NO BUCKLING

On Monday, Jonathan woke to a warm and clear Selma morning. As he headed through the Scotts' backyard to Brown Chapel, he knew that the church would be overflowing that afternoon, when King led a memorial service for Reverend Reeb. But when Jonathan reached the area of the Berlin Wall, he was shocked that it was gone. "I'm tired of hearing them sing about the damned thing," Wilson Baker grumbled. He'd cut the rope with scissors.

"The point of the wall was to make us buckle, but we didn't," said Charles Mauldin, a seventeen-year-old student leader at Hudson High School at the time. Mauldin took pride that the protesters had held their ground.

Jonathan's unflinching courage at the Berlin Wall made him well known and respected in Selma's black community. "Jonathan had a huge presence at the wall," Mauldin said.

Even more surprising than the cutting of the rope was that young blacks were shaking Baker's hand, thanking him for keeping them safe from Sheriff Clark that week. Stunned by the sudden events, Jonathan and the crowd learned more good news: they could walk to the courthouse to protest Reeb's killing. Was Selma really changing? It sure looked like it.

Jonathan had been in Selma for six days, but as he marched with a crowd to the courthouse, he knew that he'd soon have to leave. He'd already missed a week of classes and decided to drop one course. A shuttle bus from Montgomery was due in Selma that afternoon. Most of the remaining

Much of the Berlin Wall was actually a rope.

northerners planned to be on that bus and headed for flights back home.

Jonathan and Judy packed their things and stood in line for the bus, too. But Jonathan didn't feel right about leaving. What had he accomplished? There was no permission yet to march from Selma to Montgomery. Voting restrictions hadn't changed, and southern churches, including St. Paul's, were a long way from being integrated.

"There were too many white people who had just come in and were pulling out," Judy said.

Jonathan hurried to a corner store to buy cigarettes for the trip and think about what he should do. The bus pulled in and the crowd hopped on. Judy sat on their bags waiting for Jonathan.

"Are we ready to go?" Jonathan asked when he returned. But the bus had left. Had Jonathan missed it on purpose? He'd told Judy how much he wanted to stay. And she did, too.

"It was in a way kind of ridiculous," Judy explained about lining up for that bus. "After saying . . . we think this is so important, and after a week or so say, 'well, I've got more important things to do now, so long and good luck.'"

So Judy and Jonathan trudged the six blocks back to the George Washington Carver Homes and knocked on the Scotts' door.

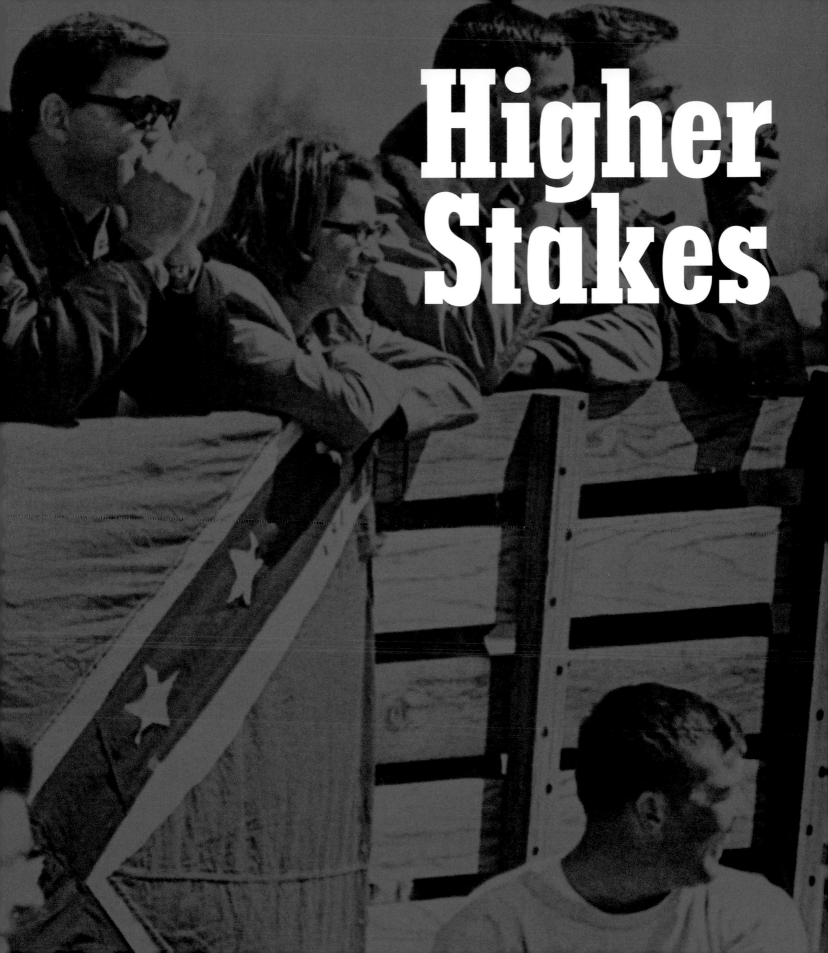

Higher Stakes

In a Selma living room, Martin Luther King Jr. watches President Lyndon Baines Johnson speak out for voting rights on March 15, 1965.

The Scotts welcomed Jonathan and Judy back. That night, friends and family crowded into the Scotts' living room, eager to watch President Lyndon B. Johnson address Congress on TV.

Spurred on by the events in Selma, Johnson wanted to let Americans know that their president wouldn't tolerate voter discrimination any longer and that he planned to stop it with a new voting rights act. The law would strip away all barriers blocking registration based on a person's race.

Believing he needed "every ounce of moral persuasion the presidency held" for the bill to pass, Johnson also hoped that his televised message would pressure Congress to put the bill into law by the summer.

"At times history and fate meet at a single time in a single place to shape a turning point in man's unending search for freedom," the president began. "So it was last week in Selma, Alabama."

In his slow Texas drawl, Johnson firmly told the seventy million Americans watching on TV what needed to be done for equal rights.

"It is wrong—deadly wrong—to deny any of your fellow Americans the right to vote in this country," Johnson said. Then, borrowing a line from Martin Luther King Jr., the president punctuated his speech by promising Americans that "We shall overcome." It was one of the most inspiring speeches ever given by an American president. Congress erupted into applause.

Jonathan cheered with the Scotts as their friends danced around the living room. A few blocks away in another home in Selma, King and John Lewis cried. As the leaders of SCLC and SNCC, they were waiting for approval to lead the march from Selma to Montgomery. Johnson's speech convinced them that it would happen soon.

As the joy from the speech died down, the Scotts told Jonathan that they were still afraid of retaliation from the sheriff's department, especially with so many white supporters leaving Selma. Bloody Sunday had shown Jonathan what the local police were capable of doing. He believed that the presence of white activists like him could help prevent brutality against blacks.

Working for social justice had become as important to Jonathan as his schooling. But if he and Judy didn't return to ETS soon, they'd fail their classes.

Eager to keep working for civil rights, they discussed what to do. "I've got a car," Judy finally said, remembering her father's red Volkswagen Beetle, which was back at ETS.

Jonathan came up with a solution. They'd complete their schoolwork correspondence-style while living in Selma. All they had to do was fly back to Cambridge, convince their professors, and pick up Judy's father's car.

The next morning, he and Judy flew to ETS and received approval to finish their schoolwork from Selma and then return to school for their May exams.

Jonathan had developed a fever from those cold, rainy nights at the Berlin Wall, but his enthusiasm ran high. "Something had happened to me in Selma which meant I had to come back," he told his professors. The treatment of Selma's blacks was the biggest injustice he'd ever seen, and

Judy Upham's red Volkswagen provided vital transportation during Jonathan's time in Alabama. He's behind the wheel in this photo.

taking action was the only option he could live with. "The stakes were too high."

But the fate of the third attempt to march from Selma to Montgomery rested in the hands of a federal judge named Frank M. Johnson. A key player in civil rights cases, his rulings would later affect several aspects of Jonathan's life. Judge Johnson ruled that Governor Wallace's vow to block the march to Montgomery was unconstitutional because it went against the First Amendment of the Constitution. Every American had the right to picket their government, the judge reminded Wallace, and the government couldn't stop them. The march would finally go on.

121

As Jonathan drove back to Selma, hoping to arrive in time to join the march, Judy reminded him that her father had let them take the car under one condition: when they arrived in Selma, they'd park it in a garage and never use it again until they drove back home. But Jonathan knew how valuable the car would be for transportation in Selma.

Needing to stay awake for his portion of the two-day drive, Jonathan pulled into an all-night southern diner for coffee. They had something to celebrate. It was March 20, Jonathan's twenty-sixth birthday.

"When I ordered the coffee, all other voices stopped," Jonathan wrote. "I turned from cold stares and fixed my gaze on a sign over the counter: ALL CASH RECEIVED FROM SALES TO NIGGERS WILL BE SENT DIRECTLY TO THE UNITED KLANS OF AMERICA. I read it again and again, nausea rising swiftly and savagely, as the suspicious counterboy spilled coffee over the cups. It was lousy coffee."

The signs of hatred continued, reinforcing for Jonathan the reasons why white civil rights volunteers were needed in the South. Nearing Montgomery, they passed a Ku Klux Klan rally, the burning crosses on the lawn still smoldering.

"WHITE TRASH"

Jonathan was rarely on time for anything, so it was no surprise that he and Judy missed the beginning of the march. They rolled into Selma on Sunday, March 21, as Martin Luther King and John Lewis led 3,200 demonstrators over the Edmund Pettus Bridge onto Highway 80 for the long and often soggy trek to Montgomery. The marchers planned to confront Governor Wallace and demand an end to police brutality and the denial of their right to vote.

Thousands gather outside Brown Chapel on March 21, 1965, for the Selma-to-Montgomery march.

Members of the Alabama National Guard protect the marchers.

Morning temperatures had plunged below freezing, but the reception from whites lining the streets was even colder. Groups stood in front of car dealerships and diners, waving Confederate flags and holding signs saying WHITE TRASH GO HOME. Jonathan had experienced white hostility toward blacks at the Berlin Wall. Now it was directed at people like him.

"This is a grim business," Jonathan concluded. "It might as well be war." But he knew it was too late to park the car at the George Washington Carver Homes and try to catch up to join the marchers. So he drove to the Scotts' house, took a nap, and kept busy setting up his library in a bedroom.

Jonathan converted the headboard into a bookshelf, but it was difficult to concentrate on studying while one of the most significant civil rights marches ever took place a few miles away. He sprang into action when a message arrived from Hudson High School senior Ron Fuller, who was trekking to Montgomery: "Bring us more comfortable shoes." The marchers had stopped for the night at a farmer's field seven miles from Selma, and many had blisters and bloody feet.

Jonathan tossed some sturdy boots into the Volkswagen and drove up Highway 80, where strands of cotton from the previous fall's harvest still clung to the roadside fields. As he reached the campsite, Jonathan quickly discovered another concern. His teenage friends confided that they were fearful of the rifle-toting National Guard men keeping watch on the ground and in helicopters rumbling above. Since Governor Wallace had refused to provide police protection, President Johnson ordered the Alabama National Guard to keep the marchers safe. But the Alabama National Guard was "all white and Klan infiltrated," Ron Fuller believed. The fear of snipers and bombs was strong.

Families watch from their porches as marchers head for Montgomery.

The students worried that the guards, accustomed to enforcing Governor Wallace's calls for segregation, could not be trusted to ensure the safety of the marchers. Jonathan agreed. He eagerly volunteered to help guard them while they slept in four giant tents. He would sleep at the Scotts' house each day, then drive to wherever the marchers spent the night.

That first evening, the 3,200 marchers ate three tons of spaghetti, cornbread, and pork and beans. They shivered as they slept, since there weren't enough blankets or sleeping bags to go around.

The next day, as the marchers reached the swamps and farmlands of Lowndes County, Highway 80 narrowed into two lanes. Three hundred people had been selected to keep walking—280 black residents of the South and 20 whites from other areas of the United States. The others returned to Selma by chartered buses. Judge Frank Johnson had ordered the reduced number of marchers because he feared that a bigger group couldn't be kept safe.

STOKING THE FIRE

Jonathan had never spent time in Lowndes County, but he knew its deadly history of racial violence. It was the bloodiest county in Alabama—where blacks had been hanged from the limbs of moss-lined oaks—and there was no widespread voting rights campaign, as there was in Selma.

Another newcomer to the area stood by the side of the highway, waiting for the marchers. Twenty-three-year-old Stokely Carmichael—a Trinidad-born New Yorker—had no intention of marching. He saw the march as a publicity stunt. He'd been assigned as SNCC's first field organizer in charge of "Bloody Lowndes," so what he wanted were names

Instead of marching
to Montgomery,
SNCC organizer
Stokely Carmichael
(left) persuaded
Lowndes County
farmers to try
to register to vote.

and addresses of the black sharecroppers lining the road to see King walk by. Signing them up would be true progress.

As the backbone of Lowndes County, those farmers made up 80 percent of the population, but not a single one of them had ever voted. Stokely intended to change that. He was convincing, smart, and a dynamic speaker like King, but none of the farmers knew about him. They asked if he worked for King. Stokely pretended that he did, realizing that if he said yes, his blank notebook would fill up with names and addresses. "Yeah, we're with Dr. King, and when the marchers go on, we'll be here," he told onlookers while shaking their hands.

Like Jonathan, Stokely was young and determined, and both of them felt an immediate kinship with Lowndes County blacks. But, deeply rooted in his faith, Jonathan believed in the power of nonviolence and integration. Stokely had witnessed the hypocritical actions of religious leaders and shunned them. He didn't believe integration would work in the South. Stokely had severed ties with any whites he'd known in the past. Within a few months, Jonathan would force Stokely to question those convictions.

STANDING GUARD

On the third night, torrential rain pelted the tents at a muddy campsite. Jonathan trudged through the oozing mud, soaked but jubilant to be participating. "I stood security guard at the encampment," he excitedly wrote to his mother, noting that the march was "enormous" and going off "quite successfully."

The marchers were exhausted and muddy, with blistered feet and aching legs. But they were totally committed to the movement, and Jonathan was proud to help keep them safe.

He'd played a bigger role at the Berlin Wall, but that was a spontaneous demonstration and the teenagers he stood with had looked to him as a leader. This march was a well-organized event of national importance, with King and Lewis in the lead, so Jonathan was happy to be a supporter.

Jonathan was also energized by a brief meeting with the most famous marcher—King himself. "I think he is a saint," Jonathan told a friend after he and King exchanged greetings.

While Jonathan held King in high esteem, white hecklers lining the route of the march saw King as a troublemaker. They despised white civil rights workers even more. "They would refer to people like Jonathan Daniels as a nigger lover," SNCC leader John Lewis said.

Except for angry whites hurling rocks over the camp's fence one time, Jonathan felt relief that his night watches were uneventful. The National Guard had kept everyone safe—sweeping fields and bridges in search of bombs.

In Jonathan's view, the final night briefly diminished the spirit of the march, as thousands of people joined the three hundred marchers on the grounds of the City of St. Jude Hospital outside Montgomery. Some of the newly arrived white students had little awareness of the significance of the march, and they were there mostly to see celebrities perform at a "Stars for Freedom" rally. "I began to feel . . . as if I were in a circus," Jonathan admitted.

"The problem is not that they're white; it's that they're immature," he said, "and obviously not indigenous." Of course, Jonathan was white, too, and not indigenous either, but he felt a strong connection to the region and the civil rights movement. He harshly judged people who were there only to see the performers, who included comedian Dick

Enthusiastic
supporters greet
the marchers
along the route
to Montgomery.

Segregationists heckle the marchers from behind a Confederate flag.

Gregory and singers Harry Belafonte, Sammy Davis Jr., and Joan Baez.

"END YOUR FEARS"

Exhausted from lack of sleep and soaked from the rain, Jonathan joined twenty-five thousand other demonstrators for the final miles of the march. The three hundred people who'd covered the entire fifty-four-mile route donned bright orange jackets and led the way.

Slipping the orange jacket over his Hudson High School sweatshirt, student leader Charles Mauldin moved to the front of the line, just as he'd done at the Berlin Wall with Jonathan. At the outskirts of Montgomery, Mauldin rushed a few hundred yards ahead of the others. "Come and march with us!" he urged the thick crowds lining the city's streets.

"It was a call to end your fears," Mauldin said. "We were elated that something very important was occurring. We wanted them to share in it, and many did."

Jonathan and Judy arrived as the massive crowd pushed toward the capitol building. They glanced up to see the Confederate flag flying on the capitol dome but not an American one.

"People lined the streets, cheering and waving," Judy wrote. "When we all marched to the statehouse, it was almost as if we were the army of liberation marching into Paris or something."

King planned to give Governor Wallace a petition demanding protection for blacks when they registered to vote. He was told that the governor wasn't inside the capitol, but King knew better. Wallace hid in his office, peeking through the venetian blinds at the huge crowd. Wallace never came out, but King gave an inspiring speech. Surrounded by so many supporters, he spoke with confidence that the president's voting rights bill would pass.

The throng of listeners cheered—inspired and confident after such a triumphant march. The integrated march had proceeded without violence and brought great attention to the civil rights movement. "I remember having the sense then—in front of the capitol—that things were going to change," said Joyce Parrish O'Neal, who had driven from Selma with her mother and sister to march the final day. Listening to King and seeing the thousands of people standing up for their rights convinced O'Neal that the movement was succeeding.

Jonathan was also impressed by King's address, which concluded with words from "The Battle Hymn of the Republic":

> *O, be swift, my soul, to answer Him!*
> *Be jubilant, my feet!*
> *Our God is marching on.*
> *Glory, hallelujah! Glory, hallelujah!*
> *His truth is marching on.*

"He is certainly one of the greatest men of our times," Jonathan told his friends. "I pray he doesn't get bumped off— the whole country needs him."

Jonathan spotted a priest who was one of his professors at ETS and requested a blessing. He knelt on the steps of the capitol and bowed his head, grateful that the march had been a huge success.

A lone white woman
stands in support
of the Selma
marchers. Most
white sympathizers
were too afraid
to speak against
segregation and risk
losing their jobs
or their homes.

Proud young
marchers approach
the Alabama
state capitol in
Montgomery.

A KLAN MURDER

Marchers rushed to find rides out of Montgomery before nightfall. Jonathan and Judy loaded the backseat of the Volkswagen with students from Hudson High, including Ron Fuller.

In Lowndes County, a truck pressed close and tailgated them. Jonathan slowed down, thinking someone in the truck might need help. But the students saw the danger. The Volkswagen's Massachusetts license plates were a magnet for Klansmen. "Speed up!" they yelled. Rifles jutted out of the truck's windows.

"Drive as fast as you can!" Fuller shouted, crouching lower in the backseat.

The truck overtook them, then drove off.

As Jonathan frantically sped toward Brown Chapel, a green Oldsmobile with Michigan plates headed in the opposite direction. The driver, thirty-nine-year-old Viola Liuzzo, was determined to shuttle as many marchers back to Selma as she could, despite the darkening skies. Liuzzo was white and the mother of five children. She'd driven from Detroit to participate in the march and had already dropped off a group at Brown Chapel. She was returning to Montgomery for more.

Nineteen-year-old Hudson High senior Leroy Moton had offered to help, jumping into the front passenger side. On a swampy stretch of Highway 80 in Lowndes County, they were overtaken by a car filled with Klansmen. One night rider rolled down his window, aimed a gun at Liuzzo, and fired. She died instantly, slumping over the wheel as the car skidded into a field.

Activist Viola Liuzzo
of Detroit, Michigan,
was killed by
Klansmen after the
Selma-to-Montgomery
march.

The Klansmen pulled up beside the car and shined their flashlights inside. Terrified and splattered with Liuzzo's blood, Moton didn't move until the Klan car left.

ENEMY LINES

As Jonathan and his passengers arrived at Brown Chapel, civil rights workers hurried to greet them, relieved that they were safe. The Volkswagen was the first car to return since Liuzzo's murder.

After Jonathan heard of Liuzzo's death, he stood guard all night in front of Brown Chapel, refusing to let the marchers inside drive back home. While they slept on the wooden pews, Jonathan watched outside for Klan cars. "Get down," he'd tell the others keeping watch if he spotted a suspicious vehicle.

Racial violence hadn't stopped because of the march. The Liuzzo killing only added to Lowndes County's bloody reputation and was the second murder of a white demonstrator in 1965. It wouldn't be the last.

Jonathan knew that he'd have to take precautions. Never again would he let a vehicle pass him on the highway. "Sometimes I think this place isn't even civilized," he wrote. "Sure is a strange country—sort of like being deep within enemy lines."

A Life
in Danger

Jonathan, Judy Upham, and a civil rights volunteer wait for word from movement organizers on the steps of Brown Chapel.

The **Jackson, Reeb,** and **Liuzzo** murders made clear the tremendous risks civil rights workers faced, but Jonathan's resolve grew deeper. With the march over, it was time to capitalize on its success.

Reverend John Morris decided that his Episcopal Society for Cultural and Racial Unity (ESCRU) needed a full-time presence in Selma. He asked Jonathan and Judy to represent the group.

With no direct ties to King's SCLC or the student-led SNCC, Jonathan had the freedom to work alongside either group. But the lack of communication among civil rights groups in Selma surprised him. At times, it seemed to Jonathan as if no one was in charge of the civil rights movement in the city. He learned about demonstrations and other events by word of mouth or signs posted at Brown Chapel and was frustrated by the lack of structure.

Jonathan was in the South to get things done. He and Judy helped register voters, tutored students, and shuttled people to doctors' appointments in the trusty Volkswagen. Every morning they said prayers with the Scott children. They stood up to police at voter registration lines.

"I've heard of the work of Jonathan Daniels," SNCC chairman John Lewis said, "nitty gritty, dirty work. It was not flashy . . . but it was work that needed to be done."

Searching for a bigger role, Jonathan seized the leadership of a local "dialogue committee," which meant that he'd be meeting with some of Selma's prominent citizens, otherwise known as the "white power structure." Here was an

143

opportunity to cause some positive change. Examining the list of names, he realized that most of them were members of St. Paul's Episcopal Church. Trying to convince Episcopalians to support the rights of their black neighbors fit squarely with ESCRU's goals.

Setting up their typewriter on the Scotts' coffee table, Jonathan and Judy typed the names on the list and where each person stood regarding integration of the city and the church. The prospect of allies looked grim:

Reverend Mathews: Nice guy but not to be trusted . . . will take a long time to overcome prejudices.

Judge Reynolds: die-hard . . . in defense of Southern way of life. Nasty to the kids in court . . . little hope of change in attitude.

Judge Bernard Reynolds was the head usher who'd prevented Jonathan from integrating the church. In his courthouse office, Reynolds had told Jonathan "the nigger trash you bring with you will *never* be accepted in St. Paul's."

Jonathan's blood boiled when he heard comments like that, but he held back his anger and asked why.

Reynolds insisted that segregation was not a sin, but God's will, and that the Bible said so. Jonathan responded that the Bible did not say that. But Reynolds grew more irritated when Jonathan challenged him. The judge said it didn't matter whether the Bible supported integration or not—it was wrong.

Jonathan vowed to stay calm. He asked how the two sides of the community could work together. But the judge claimed that blacks were treated more kindly in Selma and Dallas County than anywhere else in the country.

Jonathan took this photo of Judy Upham with Selma children at Brown Chapel. Jonathan and Judy felt safer in the city's black community.

Jonathan often learned of civil rights events from notices posted at Brown Chapel.

The real problem, he insisted, came from outside agitators like Jonathan and the federal government.

Of course, not all whites in the South opposed integration. Jonathan met with Selma whites who condemned the violence inflicted by Sheriff Clark. Their liberal thinking meant not hating, but their fear meant that they'd never push for change.

"I must confess that at this point it looks as if only a miracle or guerilla warfare will make a dent on the white community," Jonathan wrote. His frustration with the stubbornness of southern whites was increasing, and it would grow much stronger in the coming days.

CALLED TO ACTION

On Monday, April 5, Jonathan handed out sandwiches on a slow-moving voter registration line outside the courthouse in Selma. It was the type of "nitty gritty" work John Lewis described—important but not very exciting.

Word arrived of a growing conflict in the nearby farming community of Camden, where potential black voters had an even tougher time trying to register than people in Selma. Camden high school students were demonstrating for their parents' voting rights and protesting the poor conditions of their crumbling school, which was still heated by a woodstove. When Jonathan learned that the students were being harassed by police, he drove to Camden. He could accomplish more in a confrontation than he could in a sandwich line.

Jonathan brought his new "super-duper camera," which he said "cost a small fortune, but it's very fast and very accurate. We got it primarily to record violence if and when it occurs (when we're not the recipients, that is)."

R. B. Hudson High School students join hands and sing freedom songs outside Brown Chapel in defiance of police orders.

A teenage protester screams in pain after being tear-gassed by the Camden, Alabama, mayor and other city officials.

Several times in the past week, more than a hundred students had walked out of the all-black Camden high school. The students planned to march to city hall as a peaceful sign of protest. But before they reached the downtown area, Camden's pistol-toting mayor met them with a swarm of police, barring the marchers from advancing.

"I'm ready to talk to you people any time you come down to city hall like half human beings," the mayor said. "But when you come up here like a bunch of cattle, you are not going in."

A student got out of line and took a small step forward. The mayor ripped the cover off a smoke bomb and threw it, causing the kids to run. Some staggered to the ground, collapsing in pain along the road and yelling that they couldn't see.

Jonathan arrived shortly after the students regrouped outside the school. While their frightened principal sat angrily in his office, Jonathan met with the students. To earn their trust, he told them of his experiences at the Berlin Wall, where kids the same age as them had firmly held their ground and achieved results.

The Camden teenagers asked Jonathan for advice on what to do next. He reminded them that this was their demonstration and that he was willing to do what they thought was best. So the students asked Jonathan to come back the next day when they would march again.

UNDER ATTACK

Jonathan joined the group as they protested the following day. Marchers swung an American flag as they walked. The demonstration would severely test Jonathan's belief that conflicts should be approached with "'active nonresistance,' not to 'confront,' but to love and to heal and to free." Police rushed in with weapons, and Jonathan rolled to the ground in a position of nonviolence. A canister of tear gas burst open near his feet, and clouds of yellow gas filled the air. The protesters coughed uncontrollably, fighting hard not to rub their stinging eyes. Reporters and photographers captured the assault.

Jonathan had viewed Bloody Sunday's police attack on TV, but now he was in the middle of one. It enraged him, especially since the Camden teenagers had also acted in a peaceful manner.

Jonathan's skin stung with red burns from the tear gas. "I should gladly have procured a high-powered rifle and taken to the woods—to fight the battle as the Klansmen do," he admitted. "I was very, very angry with white people."

Struggling to his feet, Jonathan saw injured marchers and he abandoned hopes of making it to city hall. He ran to the Volkswagen and helped shuttle the wounded to the high school, where a first aid station was set up.

When the smoke finally cleared, Jonathan's hostility toward the police began to ease. "I saw that the men who came at me were themselves not free," he wrote. "It was not that cruelty was so sweet to them (though I'm afraid sometimes it is), *but that they didn't know what else to do.* Even though they were white and hateful and my enemy, they were human beings, too."

The students persisted, and by Friday they made a breakthrough. Photos of the peaceful demonstrators wearing suits and dresses being tear-gassed by rifle-toting police were printed in newspapers across the country. Anxious not to have another tragedy like Bloody Sunday, the Camden mayor permitted the students to march to city hall. Jonathan and five hundred other demonstrators joined them, including many of the students' parents, and the mayor agreed to let some of the parents register that day.

Distributed by:
Southern Christian Leadership Conference
Dr. Martin Luther King, Jr., President

Alabama Negroes are
"Sick and Tired of being Sick and Tired!"

[x] SICK OF BEING BEATEN, THREATENED, AND CURSED BY POLICEMEN AND SHERIFFS.

[x] TIRED OF WORKING ALL DAY IN THE SHOPS, FIELDS AND KITCHENS OF WHITE PEOPLE, DOING THE DIRTY, HARD WORK AND NOT BEING PAID ENOUGH TO FEED, CLOTHE AND HOUSE THEIR CHILDREN AND THEMSELVES RESPECTABLY.

[x] SICK OF POOR SCHOOLS THAT LEAD ONLY TO POOR JOBS.

[x] SICK OF SMELLY OUTHOUSES AND TIRED OF UNPAVED STREETS, THAT BECOME MUDHOLES WHEN IT RAINS.

[x] TIRED OF BEING RULED BY RACIST PUBLIC OFFICIALS.

[x] SICK AND TIRED OF BEING PARADED AS HALF-HUMANS, UNABLE TO GOVERN OURSELVES, EMBARRASSED, BRUTALIZED, AND INSULTED,WHEN THEY EXERCISE THEIR RIGHTS AS AMERICAN CITIZENS AND TRY TO REGISTER AND VOTE.

Let Us Move Now and Demand
the Right to Vote!

[x] DON'T WE PAY TAXES?

[x] DON'T WE RISK OUR LIVES FIGHTING IN THE UNITED STATES MILITARY?

[x] AREN'T WE CITIZENS OF DALLAS COUNTY, ALABAMA, AND THE UNITED STATES OF AMERICA?

[x] AREN'T WE AS HUMAN AS WHITE PEOPLE?

THEN WE SHOULD DECIDE WHO OUR SHERIFFS, POLICEMEN, COUNTY COMMISSIONERS, MAYORS, SCHOOL OFFICIALS AND EMPLOYERS ARE.... LET US MOVE AS CITIZENS OF ALABAMA AND DEMAND THE RIGHT TO VOTE!

Join the Movement!

This Southern Christian Leadership Conference poster urged Dallas County residents to demand the right to vote.

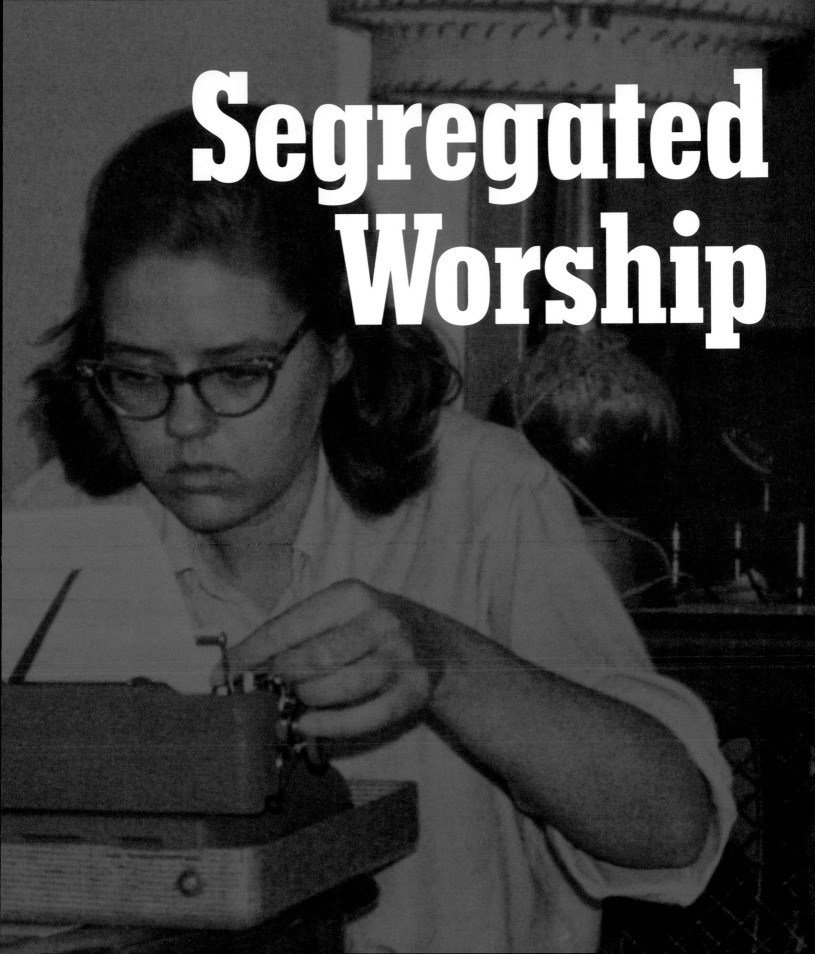

Segregated Worship

On April 11, 1965, Jonathan brought this integrated group to St. Paul's Episcopal Church in Selma. They succeeded in attending the communion service.

Jonathan's busy week was far from over. On Palm Sunday, April 11, he turned his focus to trying to fully integrate the church by attending a communion service. Jonathan, Judy, and their mixed group headed up the steps of St. Paul's—the young girls in freshly pressed dresses and Jonathan in a suit his roommate had mailed him from ETS. They stood calmly at the front doors waiting to be let in. But the ushers were more hostile than ever.

Police sirens drowned out the church bells. "They called the cops on us and refused to let us into the church," Jonathan recalled.

Surprisingly, Reverend Mathews intervened. He hurried to meet the group at the door and told the ushers the hard truth. Jonathan had been right—keeping blacks from attending the service was a violation of Episcopal law. Reluctantly, the ushers allowed them in. It had taken a month of refusals, but Jonathan's persistence paid off. He had finally integrated St. Paul's communion service.

The breakthrough was bittersweet. As an usher led them to their seats, one man couldn't control his anger. "You god-damned scum!" he shouted. The usher seated Jonathan's group in a back row, away from the white worshippers. This was another form of segregation and Jonathan recognized it. Back-of-the-bus seating didn't mean equal treatment, and Jonathan was certain who was behind the decision: Alabama's segregationist bishop, Charles Carpenter.

"This new expression of the old slave gallery must be seen for what it is—a denial of the unity of all men," Jonathan wrote angrily, naming Carpenter and emphasizing that segregated seating "must not be allowed to gain a foothold."

Jonathan felt that his church had let him and his black brothers and sisters down, but he remained committed to his faith. Around this time, he started wearing a clerical collar. "Technically we don't have such a garb or uniform for

Jonathan, Judy, and high school student Ron Fuller at a Selma gas station. "We rarely entered the white section of town on foot, and never at night," Judy said. A white gas-station attendant once loosened their tire valves so the tires would go flat.

seminarians, but it was his choice," said ESCRU's Reverend Morris, who gave Jonathan permission to wear the collar.

"You should see me in my seminarian's collar and dungaree suit!" Jonathan told a friend. "I must say, I look most proper." It was also dangerous. Other clergy involved in the civil rights movement avoided wearing their collars around whites in Alabama because they feared for their lives. Morris agreed it was important that Jonathan "be symbolically seen" as a representative of the Episcopal Church.

The reaction came quickly. A man in line at the Selma post office pointed to Jonathan's collar and the ESCRU button pinned to his jacket. "Know what he is?" the man said to his friend. "Why, he's a white niggah."

Jonathan was embarrassed to be singled out, but the incident left a lasting impression. "It is the highest honor, the most precious distinction I have ever received," he wrote. "It is one that I do not deserve—and cannot ever earn. As I type now, my hands are hopelessly white. But my heart is black."

"ECONOMIC WITHDRAWAL"

By mid-April, conditions outside the Dallas County Courthouse in Selma had improved. A judge ordered Sheriff Clark to stop harassing applicants as they waited in line to register to vote. They still needed to pass the nearly impossible literacy tests, though, so Martin Luther King encouraged a boycott of white-owned stores in an attempt to change the situation. It was announced at a mass meeting as an "economic withdrawal."

"It wasn't termed a boycott, but it was," recalled Joyce Parrish O'Neal, a junior at R. B. Hudson High School that year.

She said the attitude in the black community was that "we can hurt our tormentors if we stop giving them our money."

Blacks stayed out of white-owned businesses where they had previously shopped. "As a people, we spent money," O'Neal said, so the boycott was "very successful."

As usual, teenagers played a big role in the boycott. For example, O'Neal and other teens decided not to buy their prom dresses at local stores. An aunt sent dresses from Cleveland, Ohio, for Joyce and her sister.

Jonathan and Judy joined the boycott, too, buying food, clothing, and camera equipment in Montgomery. "I'm sorry to say that I think the boycott is really necessary," Jonathan wrote. They also stopped buying Pepsi because the Selma distributor was a member of Sheriff Clark's posse.

TARGET VEHICLE

If Jonathan's clerical collar branded him an integrationist, the red Volkswagen only made things worse. Driving back from church one time, he was slapped with a hefty speeding ticket. "Our Massachusetts plates seemed to glow in the night," he wrote. He'd been driving only thirteen miles an hour along a Selma dirt road, but the message was clear: the plates stuck out and were on the sheriff's radar.

Jonathan had seen other red Volkswagens in town with Alabama license plates, so he thought a switch might help the car blend in. He and Judy went to the courthouse, but they needed to provide a Selma address to acquire Alabama plates. Jonathan wrote the Scotts' number at the Carver Homes. He soon regretted it. Within hours, housing officials telephoned the Scotts with a warning: Their rented house

THE TROOPERS BEAT NEGROES AGAIN YESTERDAY

THE BLACKOUT IS STILL ON! DONT LISTEN TO WHITE LIES!

THIS LEAFLET MADE BY
SCLC   E.L.   GCFM
(Southern Christian   (Grenada County
    Leadership Conference)   Freedom Movr

Realizing that some members of Sheriff Clark's posse were store owners, black Selma residents boycotted their businesses.

was being watched. If the "'troublemakers'" from the North or "any of their luggage were found," the officials threatened the Scotts, they "would be thrown out in the street."

Jonathan crammed schoolbooks, clothing, the electric typewriter, and anything else he could fit into the car. "We moved out a little after midnight when the streets were dark and nearly deserted," he said, making sure that the Scotts wouldn't be evicted.

Friends of the Scotts who lived in rural East Selma took Jonathan and Judy in temporarily. But whenever Jonathan drove at night, the Volkswagen was followed. The Alabama plates hadn't worked after all.

Alonzo West realized that Jonathan was being watched. Nicknamed Lonzy, he was the father of ten-year-old Rachel, who'd stood with Jonathan at the Berlin Wall. He admired Jonathan's work and how he'd stayed on after the march to Montgomery when most northerners left. Lonzy had lost his job as a house painter when he became active in the movement.

Lonzy was concerned about Jonathan's safety and came up with a solution. He led Jonathan back to the Brown Chapel neighborhood and into his own house.

Living with the Wests at the George Washington Carver Homes would be a tight squeeze—there were ten children in the house. But Jonathan was grateful for Lonzy's generosity. He found a garage nearby to hide Judy's car at night.

Some of the West children already knew Jonathan and Judy, who'd been invited to live with them, too. They were excited to have them stay. There was one obstacle, though. Their mother, Alice.

Jonathan leans against the trusty Volkswagen at the George Washington Carver Homes in Selma.

"She had told us politely but emphatically that she didn't like white people—any white people," Jonathan said. "She knew from countless experiences that they couldn't be trusted."

Although Alice agreed to let them stay, she kept her distance. Understanding Alice's reluctance, Jonathan played ball with the West kids and took them for rides "like a big brother," one of them said.

> "We and the Negro children worshipping with us have repeatedly been the object of obscene remarks and insults."
>
> —JONATHAN DANIELS

The youngest child wasn't so sure and stayed away from Jonathan, just like her mother. But after a few days, Jonathan saw a change in the four-year-old. "[She] cupped my face with her tiny hands and kissed me," he said. "I knew something very important (and incredibly beautiful) had happened."

Seeing how happy her children were with Jonathan helped change Alice West's mind. "I got to know Jon . . . it just came easy. I didn't look at the color of his skin." Alice shed her concerns, and Jonathan and the Wests became like family.

But there was no change at St. Paul's. Every Sunday, the ushers sat Jonathan and his black friends in the last row. Why don't you just stay away, they kept asking them, and go to a Negro church?

left: **Stokely Carmichael laughs with Alice West in this photo taken by Jonathan Daniels.**

Charlene West combs Jonathan's hair as he prepares for a day in Selma. Jonathan lived with the West family for much of his time in the South.

Bishop Carpenter accused Jonathan of trying to destroy St. Paul's. Each Sunday Jonathan entered the church in his clerical collar, holding hands with black children. He made it clear that not only was he an activist and a man of faith—but also radically different from Reverend Mathews and Bishop Carpenter. "Jon was friendly with everybody—but the whites, they didn't care for him," Alice West said. "He'd try and integrate them and make peace," she added, "but the whites, they just couldn't."

Angered that the bishop hadn't taken action on the segregated seating issue, Jonathan took action himself. He wrote several letters to Carpenter demanding that the discrimination end. He also fired off a memo about his treatment at St. Paul's to every Episcopal bishop in the country. Then he drove to Birmingham and picketed in front of Bishop Carpenter's office. ESCRU's Reverend Morris and Reverend Henri Stines, a black priest, joined him. Carrying signs that read SLAVE GALLERY REVIVED and SEPARATION—SEGREGATION, they demonstrated for nearly five hours to protest the church's hypocritical policy.

What Jonathan didn't know was that Carpenter had sent copies of his letters to law enforcement officers in Selma, including Wilson Baker and Sheriff Clark. As an outside agitator, Jonathan Daniels had been someone they needed to keep an eye on. Now he became their target.

Alice West grew worried. "Sometimes I would pass people in the store and they wouldn't speak to him. They thought it was the worst thing to see him with a black family," she recalled. "I would tell him, 'Jon, be careful, look at the white man looking at you.'" But Jonathan acted as if he was unconcerned. Instead, he focused on the brutality against blacks by white southerners. "A hacked up black body was

The typewriter was meant for schoolwork, but Judy and Jonathan used it to write heated letters to Bishop Carpenter and to compose dozens of civil rights memos.

found today in a nearby county," he wrote. "I wonder how long the southern white will get away with rule by terror."

"WHO'S THIS ONE?"

One evening, the Wests took Jonathan and Judy to a popular Selma club for blacks. Jonathan noticed a young man glaring at him. Alice knew the man: Stokely Carmichael, the leader of SNCC in neighboring Lowndes County.

It wasn't the first time Stokely had noticed Jonathan. He'd seen him around Selma. "Who's this one?" he wondered. He was stunned that Jonathan had stayed in the area after the march to Montgomery.

Finally, Stokely couldn't contain his frustration and walked up to the Wests' table. "What are you doing here with them?" he demanded of Alice. "They're white people."

"Jon and Judy are my friends," Alice replied, adding that they were staying at her home. This was startling news coming from Alice, who a month before still carried a lifelong hatred of whites. "I'll pick my own friends," she informed Stokely, "and nobody'll tell me otherwise."

Alice's response jolted the SNCC leader. In Lowndes County, where Stokely had set up a voter registration campaign, friendships between blacks and whites seemed impossible. And there were definitely no white civil rights workers there.

Staring at Jonathan and his clerical collar, Stokely knew there was something about the northerner that had changed Alice West's *no white friends* policy.

Jonathan had also heard about Stokely, who'd been described to him as a black nationalist—believing more in black independence than integration. The summer before,

Stokely had refused to work with white civil rights volunteers in Mississippi. But Jonathan wouldn't permit Stokely to treat him like a racial stereotype—unfairly judging him because he was white. He challenged Stokely to let him volunteer in Lowndes County.

For Stokely, that was out of the question. "I explained to him that we would never let him work in Lowndes," Stokely said. Jonathan demanded to know why. Stokely responded that he'd be too visible as a target for racists. Less than a month had passed since the slaying of Viola Liuzzo on a Lowndes County highway. But Jonathan insisted that he could make a difference there.

Stokely didn't budge, but he was impressed by Jonathan's passion. "The special aspect of Jonathan was his insistence of doing good," Stokely recalled. "No force was going to stop him from living up to his responsibility." Including Stokely Carmichael.

Jonathan wasn't convinced that Stokely's refusal was strictly for safety reasons. But any decision about working in Lowndes County would have to wait until after May's year-end exams at ETS.

While spending fifteen-hour days fighting "the revolution," Jonathan had barely done any schoolwork and was panicking over papers and exams. "Sure have gummed up the works academically," he wrote to a friend. But he was beginning to care less about schoolwork and more about activism in "the streets."

"I think I used to want to be an academic to feed my pride," he wrote. "I haven't grown less sophisticated (I guess), but I have grown simpler—maybe because I'm tired and hungry most of the time."

To ease his academic load, Jonathan sent a letter to the dean of ETS asking if he could drop another course. But the dean told him that he was already taking the bare minimum required and if he didn't complete the three courses he'd be on academic probation.

So the following month, Jonathan and Judy drove back to Cambridge for their tests in the beat-up red Volkswagen with its orange-and-blue Alabama license plates. Sitting in the passenger's side, Jonathan wrote to a friend about his plans for the summer and the likelihood that he would return to Alabama. "Technically, I haven't made my own decision—but the chances are about a thousand to one that I'll decide to come back."

John Morris urged Jonathan to continue representing ESCRU in Alabama in whatever capacity he saw fit. In the two months he'd been in Selma, Jonathan had helped integrate St. Paul's, yet there was still work to be done: blacks could worship, but in back pews. He'd marched to Montgomery, standing watch as a security guard; been tear-gassed in Camden; and gained the respect and love of the Wests and other families at the Carver Homes.

But Jonathan noticed a disturbing trend: as progress was made by blacks in Alabama, resistance from whites grew more intense. He warned of a new danger: "No white outsider here is entirely safe—and I feel very strongly that one should make a realistic estimate of what that means. . . . The possibility of death, whether immediate or remote, cannot be a deciding factor for me."

Jonathan was now willing to defend his values with his life. "Selma, Alabama, is like all the world: it needs the life and witness of militant *saints*," he wrote.

His conviction would be put to a dire test a few months later in the deadliest county in Alabama.

SCHOOL'S OUT!

"LAYING HOOKY" FOR Freedom!

JOIN THE SELMA TO MONTGOMERY MARCH

THURSDAY, MARCH 25, 1965

10:00 A.M.

REPORT TO THE

M.I.A. OFFICE
716 DORSEY STREET

M.I.A. AFFILATE OF S.C.L.C.

Selma students missed many days of school in 1965 to participate in voting-rights demonstrations and marches.

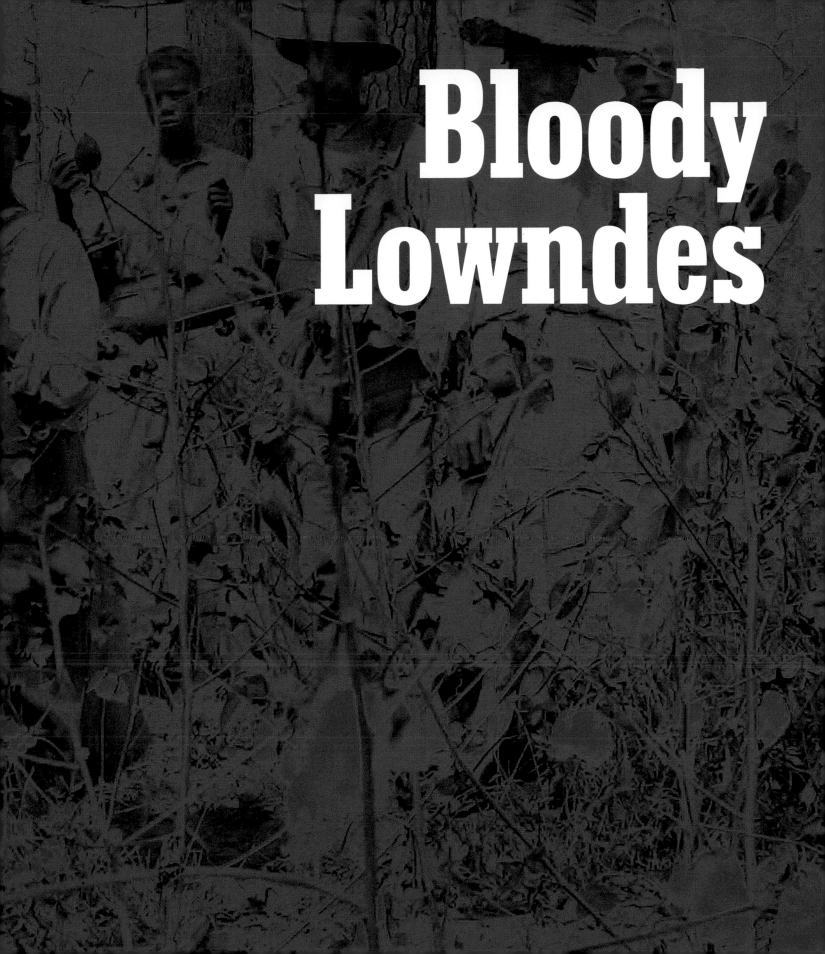

Bloody
Lowndes

Though black citizens had the constitutional right to vote in 1965 in Alabama, they were made to take a three-part literacy test in order to register. The test included reciting and writing articles on the US Constitution and answering questions about federal, state, and local government.

H aving passed his exams and with his second year at ETS over, Jonathan could fully concentrate on his activism. By Independence Day, he was back in Selma. Judy would spend the summer working at a St. Louis hospital, but she'd loaned Jonathan the Volkswagen and warned him to be careful. "I don't care if the car gets mashed up, but I'd like to see you in one piece," she wrote. "After all, you can't be replaced." Jonathan's mother and his friends were concerned. "What if you get killed?" they worried.

"If I do, it won't be because I was careless," Jonathan replied. Aware of the danger, Jonathan took out a life insurance policy. He also bought a guard dog named Thor for his mother. Jonathan's sister was married and living in New York City, so Connie Daniels was living alone.

Selma had changed in the seven weeks Jonathan was away. King's SCLC no longer had much of a presence in the city, focusing on their work from the home office in Georgia. "Atlanta's a long way off," Jonathan wrote regretfully to a classmate. King's organization had moved to other areas, focusing on better jobs for all Americans and making plans to protest the US involvement in the Vietnam War.

Jonathan arrived as a special five-day voting registration period began under Alabama law. Taking full advantage of the extra days, blacks formed long lines at the Dallas County Courthouse. Not even the cranky official who sprayed a can of deodorant in the crowded halls could discourage them. The good news was they didn't have to face the wrath of Sheriff Clark. The ongoing federal injunction kept him from beating or harassing potential voters. The bad news was they still faced a literacy test, though it was a shorter version. More than one thousand black voters registered during the extended period.

The most obvious difference to Jonathan was how few white civil rights workers were there. "You didn't have hundreds . . . , you had pockets—four here, five here, six there," SNCC's John Lewis recalled.

With so few white activists committed to working in Alabama, ESCRU's John Morris was grateful that Jonathan continued to represent the organization. Jonathan had complete authority to decide where he'd be most effective that summer. "I trusted him and his judgment," Morris said.

Jonathan had witnessed the impoverished conditions rural blacks lived in near Selma. He'd briefly stayed with a family there after fleeing from the Scotts' home back in April. Now he planned to scour the East Selma countryside, documenting the living conditions and needs of black residents. He'd present his findings to the Dallas County welfare agency to pressure the agency into offering services to the residents. But there was one hitch—Jonathan had to take along an assistant, assigned by Reverend Morris.

A NEW AGITATOR

Nineteen-year-old Marc Oliver, a surfer from San Diego, stood nervously in a Selma phone booth fumbling for the piece of paper in his pocket. At five o'clock in the morning, with the sky an inky blue, the burly white college student was sweating in his suit and tie. It wasn't because of the heat. The son of activist parents, he'd briefly visited Alabama in March for the final day of the Selma-to-Montgomery march.

Oliver vowed to come back in the summer, and he was making good on that promise.

Reverend Morris—a family friend—arranged a contact and an assignment. But the Greyhound bus dropped Oliver off in downtown Selma earlier than scheduled. The cafe across the street was open, so he hauled his luggage through the door as the smell of biscuits, sausages, and grits filled the air. But he lost his appetite after taking a stool at the counter.

"I realized I was probably in the wrong spot," Oliver said. "The waitress kept referring to the guy on my left as 'Sheriff' and then somebody called 'Jim.'" Realizing he was sitting next to Sheriff Clark—the man he'd watched on TV chasing the battered protesters back to Brown Chapel on Bloody Sunday—Oliver rushed to a phone booth. He was anxious to call the name and number on the piece of paper: Jonathan Daniels.

"Marc, it's so early, where are you?" Jonathan asked, still groggy from sleep.

"I'm in the Silver Moon Cafe."

"Jesus," Jonathan exclaimed, knowing Reverend Reeb had been killed in front of the very same cafe and figuring that Oliver had already been labeled an outside agitator within minutes of arriving in Selma.

"I'll be right there," Jonathan promised. He sped to the restaurant.

Oliver vowed to be more careful, but Jonathan wasn't thrilled to be working with an inexperienced teenager who might ruin the ambitious project he'd planned for East Selma. Fortunately, Jonathan would also be working with thirty-one-year-old Eugene Pritchett—a Selma-born SNCC

After realizing he was eating breakfast alongside Sheriff Clark, California teenager Marc Oliver made a panicked early morning call to Jonathan from the Silver Moon Cafe.

worker who more than made up for Oliver's greenness. Well known in East Selma, Pritchett earmarked fifteen cases he thought had the best chances of being accepted by the welfare agency. They loaded notebooks and a tape recorder into the car and drove into the countryside.

Marc Oliver, Eugene Pritchett, and Jonathan prepare for a long day's work in East Selma.

MAKING A DIFFERENCE

"This is Jonathan Daniels," Jonathan announced confidently into the microphone of a tape recorder, "in East Selma talking with women in especially poverty-stricken areas who are not receiving welfare assistance for one reason or another, and who are in extreme need."

As the first woman to be interviewed stared nervously at the tape recorder, Jonathan assured her, "Forget about that, don't worry about it. Talk."

Jonathan and Pritchett asked direct questions and received honest answers. Many of the women believed that social assistance and health clinics were for whites only, or they didn't know why their benefits had suddenly been cut off.

But it's what Jonathan saw, not what he heard, that shocked him more. Taking his camera everywhere he went, Jonathan snapped photos showing the poverty plaguing rural Dallas County: Many homes had no heat, so tenants wedged mattresses against walls for insulation. Children played on porches that had rotted-out floorboards, and many of them were malnourished and sick.

"What kind of water supply do you have?" Jonathan asked a woman. She ushered him outside and pointed to a pump—a shared water source that the entire community relied on. It ran through a dump yard steaming with heaps of rotting trash.

"Do you think that's a good place for it?" Jonathan asked.

"No, I don't think it is," the woman replied.

"I don't either," Jonathan said. He collected some of the water to have it tested.

While Jonathan conducted another interview, a woman rushed over to report that she'd been fired unfairly from her job that morning.

In 1965, when Jonathan took this photo, renters lived in deplorable conditions in East Selma.

Jonathan was alarmed to find this community water pump alongside a steaming town dump.

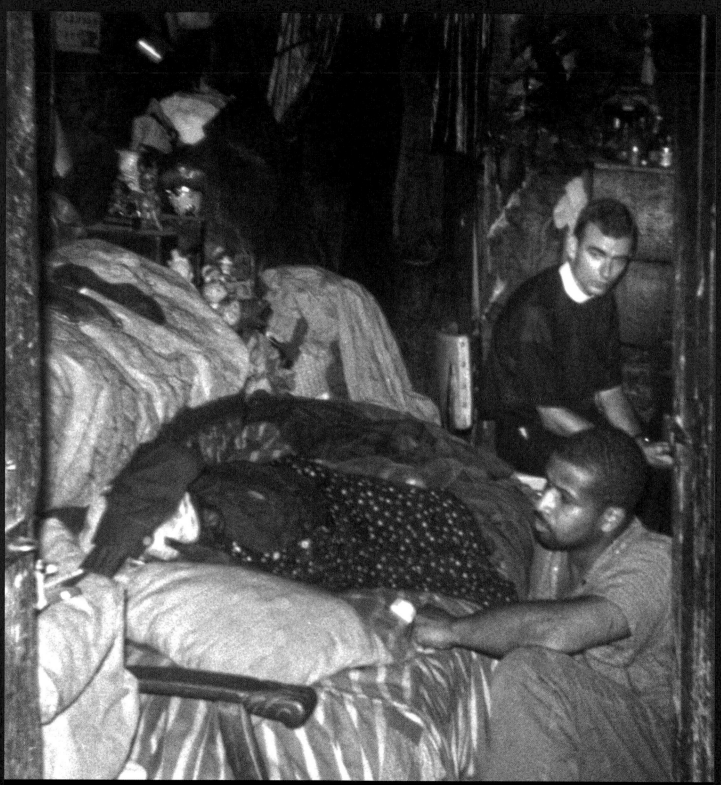

Jonathan Daniels and Eugene Pritchett documented the living conditions of dozens of East Selma citizens who resided in cramped houses.

"This interruption is to record some evidence from Lowndes County," Jonathan said into the microphone. As he adjusted the volume, the woman explained that she'd gone to Hayneville to clean a house, as she always did. But she'd been fired by the owner, Tom Coleman, who was retaliating because he'd heard that the woman's daughter had attended a speech by Martin Luther King. Coleman warned her that her home might be burned down. "Mr. Coleman, he's the one told me how he wasn't putting out them threats himself," she said nervously, "but he say I liable to get bombed."

The woman had good reason to be afraid of fifty-four-year-old Tom Coleman. He'd killed a black prison convict in 1959, claiming self-defense. Coleman was a state highway department engineer who considered himself a special deputy sheriff. His job included the supervision of convicts who were part of highway work crews. Coleman claimed that the convict had threatened him with a stolen nightstick and broken bottles. He shot the man with a 12-gauge shotgun.

Jonathan had no idea of Coleman's violent past. He and Pritchett urged the woman to report Coleman's threat to the police. Then they continued with their other interviews.

When the results of the water test came back, it revealed that the tainted dump water was the main cause of sickness in the East Selma children who lived nearby.

Jonathan couldn't convince the Dallas County authorities to make changes to the water system or the location of the city's dump yard. He did persuade the mothers to take their children to a health clinic, though. He and Pritchett also created a directory of public assistance resources, which they handed to every resident they visited.

Jonathan cared deeply about the residents of East Selma and snapped poignant photos of each family he interviewed.

Memorandum   Selma, Alabama   July 30, 1965

From: J. Daniels (Episcopal Society for Cultural & Racial Unity)
      E. Pritchett (Student Non-Violent Coordinating Committee)

To: Dallas County Residents in Need of Public Assistance

Concerning: Community Resources for Public Assistance

        The following material is a brief digest of information con-
cerning some of the community (county-state-federal) resources available to you if you need help and are not in a position to provide it
for yourself or your family. You will find below a list of the
agencies which exist to help you, the locations where you may find
them, and the hours when they are open to serve you.

        Each agency is listed by name, with a short description of the
assistance it furnishes and the conditions you must meet in order to
be eligible. In addition, you will find a list of persons familiar
with your neighborhood problems whom you may contact for advice
concerning your needs.

1. DALLAS COUNTY DEPARTMENT OF PENSIONS & SECURITY ("Welfare")

   This agency serves a number of categories of persons-in-need.
   Each category has its own conditions for eligibility, so you will
   find the several programs broken down separately. All of the
   programs operate from the same office, which is centrally located
   downtown at 108 Church Street (a big white building, with columns,
   which used to be a funeral home). The office is open Monday
   through Friday from 9:00 a.m. - 12:00 a.m. and from 1:00 p.m. -
   5:00 p.m. When you enter the building (right-hand side door as
   you face the building), you will meet a receptionist in the
   waiting room, who will make whatever arrangements are necessary
   before you interview the case-worker assigned to you.

   a. AID TO THE BLIND: The applicant must be 16 or over, in need of
      assistance, and not living with a husband or wife capable of
      providing support. The applicant must not be living in a
      public institution, receiving care and treatment for tuber-
      culosis or mental illness in any medical institution, or
      receiving any other form of aid from the Department of Pensions
      & Security. The quantity of financial assistance approved for
      the applicant will depend upon the applicant's needs and upon
      the amount of money the Department has available. More
      specific information will be provided by the Department upon
      application.

   b. AID TO THE PERMANENTLY & TOTALLY DISABLED: The applicant must
      be permanently and totally disabled and within the ages of
      18 and 64 (inclusive). Otherwise, conditions are similar to
      those above.

   c. OLD AGE PENSION: The applicant must be 65 or older. Other-
      wise, see above.

   d. MEDICAL ASSISTANCE FOR THE AGED: This program provides 15 days
      hospital care in one fiscal year for acute illness or major
      injury and a limited number of office visits to a physician for
      follow-up care within 30 days after hospitalization under this
      program. The applicant must be 65 or older and cannot be
      receiving an old age pension. Otherwise, see above.

   e. AID TO DEPENDENT CHILDREN: Eligible children must be under 18,
      without parents who can support them (even occasional visits
      by a wandering husband or boyfriend will in most cases dis-
      qualify you for support under this program -- as, of course,
      will continued pregnancies). Parents must work when they are
      physically and mentally able to do so, as must older children
      (without violating child labor laws or interfering with school
      attendance). Mothers of families deserted by a father or
      fathers are reminded that they can and should file complaints

(continued on Page 2)

By the end of July, with his work in East Selma wrapped up, Jonathan was ready for another challenge. "The faith with which I went to Selma has not changed," he wrote; "it has grown." He intended to put that faith to work in nearby Lowndes County, where conditions were even worse.

KLAN TERRITORY

Lowndes County was 725 rugged square miles of farmland threaded by single-lane dirt roads rimmed with snake-infested swamps thick with kudzu. The two main towns—Fort Deposit and the county seat of Hayneville—were specks on the map compared with Selma's downtown. And while Selma's blacks demonstrated vigorously for their rights, no one dared to demonstrate in Lowndes County.

Lowndes seemed stuck in a different time. African Americans outnumbered whites four to one, and most of them worked as sharecroppers on converted plantations. Conditions on those white-owned farms weren't much better than they were before the Civil War. "We were the type of family that had to work in the fields, I mean pick cotton like slavery time," said Geraldine Logan, an Alabama State College student from Lowndes.

Many farms didn't have phones, running water, or electricity. Few blacks owned stores, and most of the white-owned establishments forced blacks to enter through back entrances. The exceptions were places like Varner's Cash Store in Hayneville, a grocery store whose white owner had no problem having blacks enter through her front doors.

Jonathan and Pritchett created this first listing of social services available to all Dallas County residents. They distributed it widely.

In 1965, Lowndes County, Alabama, was the poorest county in the United States. Many of the residents picked cotton on white-owned plantations.

Alabama Ku Klux Klansmen burn a giant cross in 1965.

If anyone complained about the situation in Lowndes, news ripped through the county like a lightning bolt. Retaliation often came in the form of a burning cross in front of that person's home as a first warning, courtesy of the Ku Klux Klan.

As for voting, no Lowndes County black had cast a ballot in the twentieth century. Voter fraud was notorious in the county, where the names of dead people were kept on the polls. One report stated that 117 percent of white voters were registered, an impossible number. Whites feared that even a modest percentage of black voters could forever change their way of life.

No white civil rights activist had been assigned to Lowndes. Jonathan was determined to be the first, but he'd face stiff resistance from white segregationists. "The thought of integration was just intolerable to them," said one volunteer. In their eyes, having a white person support blacks meant treason to the white race.

Jonathan's hope seemed far-fetched. How could a young white man knock on the doors of black farmers and convince them to vote? The farmers had good reasons not to trust whites.

Blacks who tried to register to vote were refused at the Lowndes County Courthouse. Instead, they were made to register at the old Hayneville jail, where a gallows reminded them of earlier hangings as they tried to concentrate on the literacy test. Schoolteacher Sarah Logan, Geraldine's mother, took the test several times but was always told she'd failed. Hulda Coleman—the superintendent of schools and Tom Coleman's sister—had Sarah fired from her teaching job for trying.

In 1965, it took courage for blacks to register to vote in Alabama. Seventy-six-year-old Fannie Robertson was made to take the literacy test in the Lowndes County jail.

Stokely Carmichael was slowly changing things. Visiting farms by car or on a mule, SNCC's Lowndes County supervisor convinced a growing number of blacks to register. He and his field secretaries reinforced a small, grassroots movement started by John Hulett called the Lowndes County Christian Movement for Human Rights. Hulett had made history by becoming the county's first black to register.

By July, sixty-four blacks had succeeded by overcoming obstacles like the so-called literacy test, a poll tax, and the need to have a registered voter vouch for them. Seven hundred had failed.

Stokely Carmichael sometimes traveled from farm to farm in Lowndes County on the back of a mule.

DANGEROUS CONDITIONS

Every time a member of the SNCC team turned onto one of the dirt roads jutting through Lowndes County, their lives were in danger. It wasn't safe to have an office in Lowndes either, so they used SNCC's office in Selma when they could get a ride there.

Stokely sometimes slept in a small, four-room house outside of Hayneville owned by black farmers Mathew and Emma Jackson. They called it the Freedom House. But Stokely didn't want Klansmen knowing where he lived, so he never stayed in one place for long. And he felt certain that a white civil rights worker would attract even bigger trouble. It would be difficult for Jonathan to convince him, but Jonathan was determined to try.

Jonathan started hanging out at the Holiday Inn in Selma, knowing Stokely went there some evenings. It was the only white-owned hotel where a mixed group could meet, and it was also air-conditioned—a welcome break from the heat. Or he'd go to the Chicken Shack restaurant, where Stokely and other SNCC workers like Ruby Sales sometimes relaxed after a long day in Lowndes.

Ruby was a petite seventeen-year-old Tuskegee Institute student from Georgia. Born into a middle-class family and raised at the integrated army base of Fort Benning, where her father was an officer, Ruby was unaccustomed to brutality against her race. Stunned to experience it firsthand after joining a Tuskegee student protest in Montgomery in early March, she left school to work in Lowndes County. But if being a male SNCC worker in Lowndes was treacherous, being a teenage black woman was even scarier, and Ruby soon received death threats. She was effective at her job but developed ulcers because of the stress.

Stokely often worked at the SNCC office on Franklin Street in Selma. SNCC worker Willie Vaughn waits while Stokely makes a call.

Stokely Carmichael and Ruby Sales canvassed the Lowndes County countryside with Jonathan, encouraging farmers to register for voting.

Ruby was a compelling motivator, which made her valuable for stirring up enthusiasm. "I was a person who could get large numbers of people to go to mass meetings," she said. That made her a target.

For Ruby, talking about philosophy at the Chicken Shack with Jonathan offered a welcome relief from the pressure. They quickly became friends. "He understood that the questions of democracy were as important to him as they were for us, and that's what made him unique," Ruby explained. "He would say, 'We're in this struggle together.'"

But Ruby and the other SNCC workers refused to let Jonathan work in Lowndes. "It was a pragmatic question of, 'Would his being there jeopardize the actions and put people at risk?'" Ruby said. "Jonathan could be very defiant. His even wanting to be in Lowndes County was an act of defiance, because we didn't want him there."

"STAY THE HECK AWAY"

Jonathan found an ally in Lowndes County SNCC volunteer Gloria Larry. The University of California, Berkeley, graduate student had left school to join the movement after seeing a photo of murdered civil rights workers James Chaney, Andrew Goodman, and Michael Schwerner, who'd been killed in Mississippi the previous summer. Shocked by the "picture of the bodies being put into black plastic bags," she decided "that it was more important to be down South and part of the struggle than to be in school."

When Gloria mentioned to Jonathan that she was an Episcopalian, he told her about his efforts at St. Paul's. She and Jonathan started attending Sunday services together

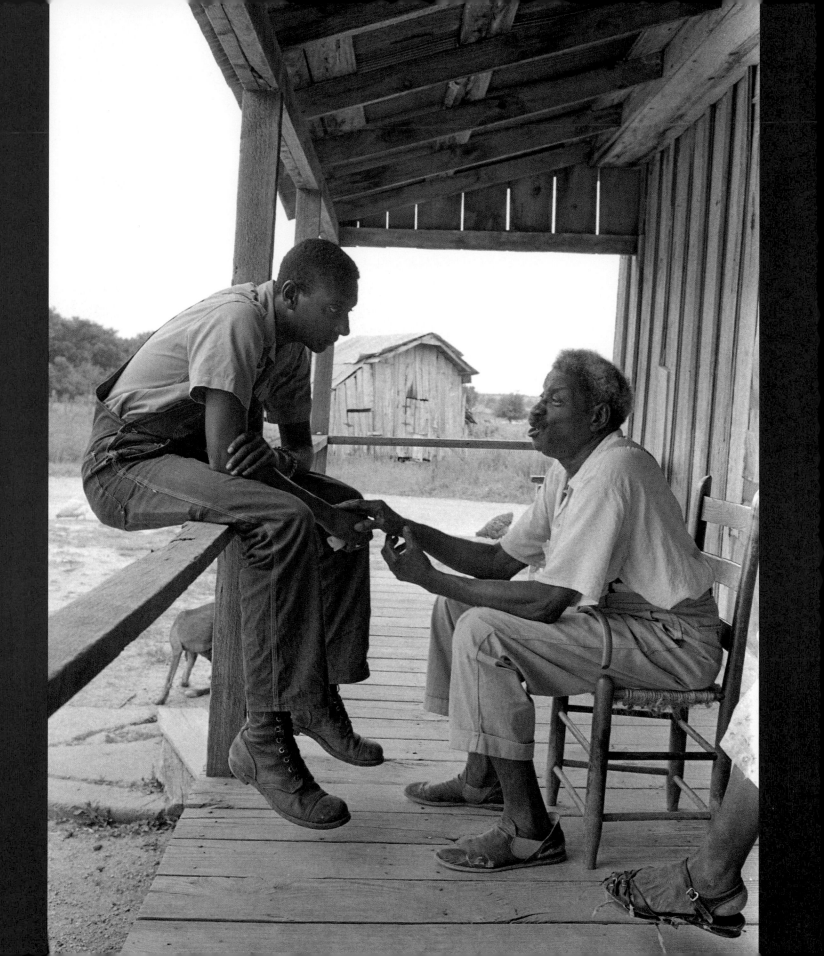

and bringing the West children along. Though still treated with hostility, they kept St. Paul's integrated.

Stokely Carmichael spent his Sunday nights in Lowndes County's black churches, drumming up support at mass meetings that Ruby convinced residents to attend. Jonathan urged Stokely to let him attend one of those meetings.

Stokely knew of Jonathan's strong record in Selma— forcing integration of the church, urging blacks to take advantage of social services, and protesting with teens. Stokely hesitated, then yielded slightly.

"I may have said he could probably come with Gloria and them to a meeting, but they'd have to return to Selma that same night," Stokely recalled. "What I should have said very firmly was, please, stay the heck away from Lowndes."

left: **Stokely convinced eighty-two-year-old Lowndes County farmer Jack Crawford to register.**

"I bought a super-duper camera," Jonathan wrote to a friend. **"It cost a small fortune, but it's very fast and very accurate. We got it primarily to record violence if and when it occurs (when we're not the recipients, that is)."**

Stripped
of Color

VOTING

What is the vote?

VOTING IS THE WAY A CITIZEN CHOOSES PEOPLE TO REPRESENT HIM IN HIS COUNTY, STATE AND FEDERAL GOVERNMENT. WHEN A CITIZEN VOTES, HE SPEAKS FOR HIMSELF ABOUT THINGS THAT CONCERN HIS OWN WELFARE.

Why vote?

IF YOU DON'T VOTE, YOU GIVE UP YOUR RIGHT TO DECIDE FOR YOURSELF HOW YOU WANT THINGS TO BE DONE IN YOUR GOVERNMENT. YOUR VOICE NEVER GETS HEARD IN POLITICS IF YOU DON'T VOTE.

How does voting work?

FIRST, YOU HAVE TO BE REGISTERED. THIS MEANS YOU HAVE TO GO TO HAVE YOUR NAME PUT ON A LIST ALONG WITH OTHERS WHO WANT TO VOTE IN ELECTIONS IN YOUR COUNTY OR STATE. THEN YOU MUST PAY THE POLL TAX.

Can YOU vote?

YES. ANY PERSON CAN BE A QUALIFIED VOTER IF HE OR SHE IS AT LEAST 21 YEARS OLD, HAS LIVED IN THE STATE AT LEAST ONE YEAR, IN THE COUNTY SIX MONTHS AND IN THE PRECINCT THREE MONTHS.

Looking for another way to test the racial barriers, Jonathan drove Marc Oliver and some of the West children to see the movie *The Sandpiper* in downtown Selma. The city's theaters allowed blacks to enter, but seating was strictly segregated. The Civil Rights Act of 1964 had banned segregation in public places, but businesses in Selma regularly ignored that law. Jonathan parked in front of the Wilby Theatre. When they entered the crowded lobby, Oliver and the kids headed up the stairs to the balcony meant for blacks. That didn't suit Jonathan. "Downstairs," he told them, unhappy about the inequity and ready to argue.

Jonathan led the way to the middle seats. "He was fearless," Oliver said. "He was not afraid of confrontation—he saw it as one of the best tools for social change."

An usher approached the group and asked them to leave. Jonathan refused. "We bought a ticket, we're admitted, we're staying," he insisted. Whites started clearing out of their seats in the rows around them as the lights dimmed.

Worried about potential violence after the movie, Oliver made Jonathan promise that they'd leave early. But the movie held their attention and they stayed until the end. By the time they got into the Volkswagen, it had been blocked by another car. Knowing they'd soon be surrounded by an angry group of whites, Jonathan hopped the curb, drove along the sidewalk, and sped through alleys and red lights until he felt certain they weren't being followed and could return home safely.

INFIGHTING

Oliver left after only two weeks in Selma, but that was enough time for him to grow uneasy about Jonathan's future plans. "Jon was beginning to develop a stronger interest in Lowndes County," he recalled, "and was being asked to go out there some more." Few of the SNCC workers owned cars, so Jonathan was frequently asked to transport them from Selma to Lowndes. "Jon was always available and willing," Oliver said.

Oliver agreed with SNCC's rule of having "no white presence" in Lowndes. "That county was so violent and so rigid that there'd be no liaisons made in the white community like we had in Selma," he said.

Oliver had also been surprised to discover prejudice in SNCC. He "found within the SNCC movement strong tendencies towards black nationalism and resentments to whites, even whites working in the movement," he said. "It took Jon quite a while to be accepted by SNCC."

One night at the Chicken Shack, Jonathan and Stokely debated about race relations. "The day may come that you and I will be on the opposite ends of the pole," Jonathan told Stokely. "We'll be fighting each other, because if you are really serious about your tendencies towards black nationalism, I'll end up standing against you like I stand against the Klan."

Stokely listened intently, then nodded. Jonathan kept pushing to be part of SNCC's efforts in Lowndes County, despite the fact that his seminarian collar would make him a target for racists and that SNCC leaders didn't want him there.

"Look, if you come to Lowndes County you'll just get shot," Stokely argued.

Jonathan's reaction was harsh. He'd clearly demonstrated his commitment to equal rights. Now Stokely was denying him an opportunity simply because of the color of Jonathan's skin. "You're a racist," Jonathan replied.

That caught Stokely off guard. "Oh, don't hand me that," Stokely said. "You going to tell me just because—"

Jonathan cut him off. "No, you can get killed!" he said. "You think you can't get killed?"

"Of course I can get killed," Stokely replied.

"So you just want you to get killed, you don't want me to get killed," Jonathan said.

"All right, all right, I see your point," Stokely admitted. He hadn't believed that a white person could be as committed to civil rights as a black one—that Jonathan would actually put his life on the line. It wasn't that Jonathan or Stokely intended to be killed, but that Jonathan was just as willing to take the risk as Stokely. "Not the usual white liberal arguments," admitted Stokely, who'd seen too many white volunteers flee from confrontations.

Jonathan had finally convinced Stokely to let him work in Lowndes. "We were so close in our thinking," Stokely said. "See, Jon went beyond civil rights. He went to man's inhumanity to man, stripped of color."

Now Stokely had to sway Ruby Sales and the others.

Stokely "made us change our minds," Ruby explained. "He said, 'You can't . . . get angry with white people when you're doing the same thing.'"

The following day, Jonathan became the first white volunteer in SNCC's drive in Lowndes County. Excited, he woke up early, put on his freshly pressed jeans and seminarian collar, and hopped into his car. He intended to reach as many farmers as he could before they headed to the fields under the scorching August sun. He and Willie Vaughn, a young Mississippi SNCC worker, combed southern Lowndes, urging black residents to register to vote.

But the sharecroppers were wary. When Jonathan knocked on their doors or greeted them in the fields, their first reaction was fear. He was asking them to risk their jobs and even their lives to register. But Jonathan's sincerity and enthusiasm earned their trust. They knew he was risking his life, too.

"I was totally free—at least free to give my life, if that had to be," Jonathan wrote. "[With] my black brothers at my side, there was no longer anything to fear in all of Creation except my own blindness."

JOKES AND HOPE

Sometimes Jonathan and Vaughn drove farmers to the Hayneville jail to register to vote, then they'd buy a cold soda at Varner's Cash Store. On other days, Jonathan spoke with farmers in their barns about applying for loans through a federal farming program.

During the long days, Jonathan's joy infected the SNCC workers who rode around with him in the Volkswagen. They introduced him to people in the county.

"You're riding in a car with someone, and . . . you know your life is in danger, but that person is cracking jokes and you're laughing, and suddenly the space seems bearable," said Ruby. "Of course my resistance against his being there melted . . . and I forgot about the danger," she added. "Whenever I looked in Jonathan's eyes I always felt the possibility of hope."

Jonathan often canvassed with Stokely, who was impressed by his new friend's sincerity and courage. "One of the reasons most people liked him was that he was unafraid," Stokely said. Traveling from farmhouse to farmhouse, they were always hungry. So they'd pluck cucumbers right out of the dirt, barely dusting them off before devouring them. "I'm starved most of the time," Jonathan admitted.

Stokely meets a Lowndes County farmer in July 1965. Jonathan canvassed with Stokely many times that summer.

SHERIFF

②

The sheriff keeps the peace in the country.

③

He suppresses riots

④

unlawful assembly

⑤

and stops fights

I NEED FIVE MEN!

WE WILL HE

HE CAN HAVE A POSSE.

Jonathan felt more grounded in the black community than with white people in the South. He didn't see his efforts as missionary work or charity; he was working with people that he saw as his equals. But they weren't being treated as equals, and he intended to change that.

Jonathan and Stokely handed out comic books SNCC had created—illustrating how county government operated and reminding farmers of the power of the ballot. If enough blacks voted, they could elect people who would put an end to the cycle of corruption that kept blacks repressed. But encouraging blacks to put their fears aside and try to register proved difficult.

There was another reason why SNCC workers rushed to register as many blacks as possible: Lowndes County voting registrar Carl Golson had temporarily eliminated the literacy test.

"LOWNDES COUNTY WAS MARS"

Golson was shocked by the developments in Lowndes County's black community, and his resentment toward "outside agitators" like Stokely and Jonathan grew deeper. But Golson despised federal interference even more. Anticipating that the voting rights bill would soon pass, federal registrars warned Golson that if he didn't start registering more blacks, they would do it for him. In an attempt to stop the feds from coming, Golson ended the literacy test.

Jonathan and the SNCC workers moved quickly to take advantage of the change to the registration system, working from dawn until late into the night. They didn't trust that the federal registrars would actually come to Lowndes County, because the feds had never paid attention to the shockingly low numbers of black voters before. "The Justice Department's record in the South is very bad," said a SNCC official. They also expected that Golson would eventually bring back the literacy tests—especially if federal officials didn't show up.

Jonathan's deeper involvement in Lowndes County alarmed his friends, including Marc Oliver. A week after Oliver had left Alabama, his heart sank as he read the last line of a letter from Jonathan: "I'm spending more time working out in Lowndes County with Stokely and SNCC," Jonathan wrote, "though ultimately I'm sure you'd disagree profoundly."

Oliver did disagree. "I knew how dangerous that was," he said. "Selma was dangerous. Lowndes County was Mars." Oliver couldn't believe that SNCC's policy of keeping a low profile in Lowndes had suddenly changed. But he didn't hear from Jonathan again.

What Jonathan had failed to write to Oliver was that he'd brought about the change in SNCC policy himself. But Stokely was right; the hostility in Lowndes was increasing because of Jonathan's presence. "If you are white in this struggle, you were on the front line everywhere, all the time," Stokely explained. "Even when with us, there would not be a retreat, because he couldn't lose himself among the people as we could." Jonathan did not blend in.

Neither did his car, which was too recognizable and too slow for safety in Lowndes. So Jonathan convinced ESCRU's Reverend Morris to rent him a vehicle with more horsepower than Judy's Volkswagen. Not only was Jonathan a target, but in Lowndes County he was now being chased. What's more, he'd been told that a group of men were knocking on doors looking for him.

Jonathan felt certain that his rented white Plymouth Fury could elude any Klan night riders intent on running him down. The car was put to the test soon after, when Rabbi Harold Saperstein and his wife, Marcia, arrived as volunteers.

Rabbi Harold Saperstein spent a week in August 1965 working with Jonathan in Lowndes County.

Rabbi Saperstein didn't expect to see that kind of vehicle or the clothes that his seminarian contact in Selma wore. "He was a good looking young man, with an eager face," Saperstein remembered. "I looked down and was startled to see that he was wearing blue jeans, but meticulously clean and pressed."

As head of Temple Emanu-El of Lynbrook, Long Island, fifty-five-year-old Rabbi Saperstein was a well-respected member of New York State's Jewish community. He'd served as a US Army chaplain in Europe during World War II, witnessing the liberation of several concentration camps. Now he and Marcia had volunteered for a week in Alabama.

Like Jonathan, Rabbi Saperstein saw the hypocrisies within his own religious community when it came to segregation, and he was disappointed that most of Selma's Jews were not actively working toward integration. He asked Jonathan if he and Marcia could accompany him to Lowndes. They headed into the countryside along with another SNCC worker.

At the Lowndes County Courthouse in Hayneville, the Sapersteins immediately saw how whites in the county felt about blacks voting. Segregationists had painted swastikas on a water tower behind the courthouse, and the charred remains of burning crosses damaged lawns nearby. But their spirits rose when they saw Jonathan in action, impressed by his easy rapport with the sharecroppers. "He spoke to them as human being to human being without condescension—without superiority—and at the same time without artificial goodwill," the rabbi said.

Saperstein said the mood turned from calm to terror as they approached another farm to encourage sharecroppers to register. "As we pulled up, an insurance collector drove up the road," Saperstein recalled. Recognizing the man as a Klan member, Jonathan veered off the road and onto another one. He sped toward the highway. But "a couple miles down the road we found ourselves practically blocked by a highway maintenance truck," Saperstein said.

Rabbi Saperstein photographed this swastika outside the Lowndes County Courthouse when he arrived in Hayneville with Jonathan.

President Lyndon Baines Johnson reaches to shake hands with Martin Luther King Jr. after signing the Voting Rights Act of 1965. Johnson presented the pen he used to King.

Too late to turn back, they were forced to stop. Four menacing men got out of the truck. Saperstein and his wife held their breaths, thinking they were about to be murdered. One of the men approached the Fury and peered inside. Surprised to see Marcia, the man hesitated, then walked away. But Rabbi Saperstein never forgot the man's angry face.

Jonathan rushed back to Selma at more than ninety miles an hour while the Sapersteins prayed in the backseat. "You're a madman," Saperstein told him.

"The first rule of driving in Lowndes County is that no car must ever pass you," Jonathan replied.

When Stokely heard about the incident, he wasn't surprised. "Jon was a dangerous fellow," he said. "He was living a life that would threaten the very existence of the political structure in Alabama."

THE RIGHT TO VOTE

On Friday, August 6, things weren't proceeding the way Lowndes County registrar Carl Golson had hoped. In Washington, DC, John Lewis and Martin Luther King stood in the President's Room of the US Capitol as President Johnson signed the Voting Rights Act into law, eliminating the barriers that made it so difficult for blacks to register.

Federal registrars informed Golson that their team was headed to Lowndes County and would begin registering black applicants on Tuesday morning. The FBI would be there, too, in case there was trouble.

Golson was furious. "We lived up to our agreement, but they broke theirs," he fumed, believing he had more than cooperated with the federal government when he halted the literacy tests.

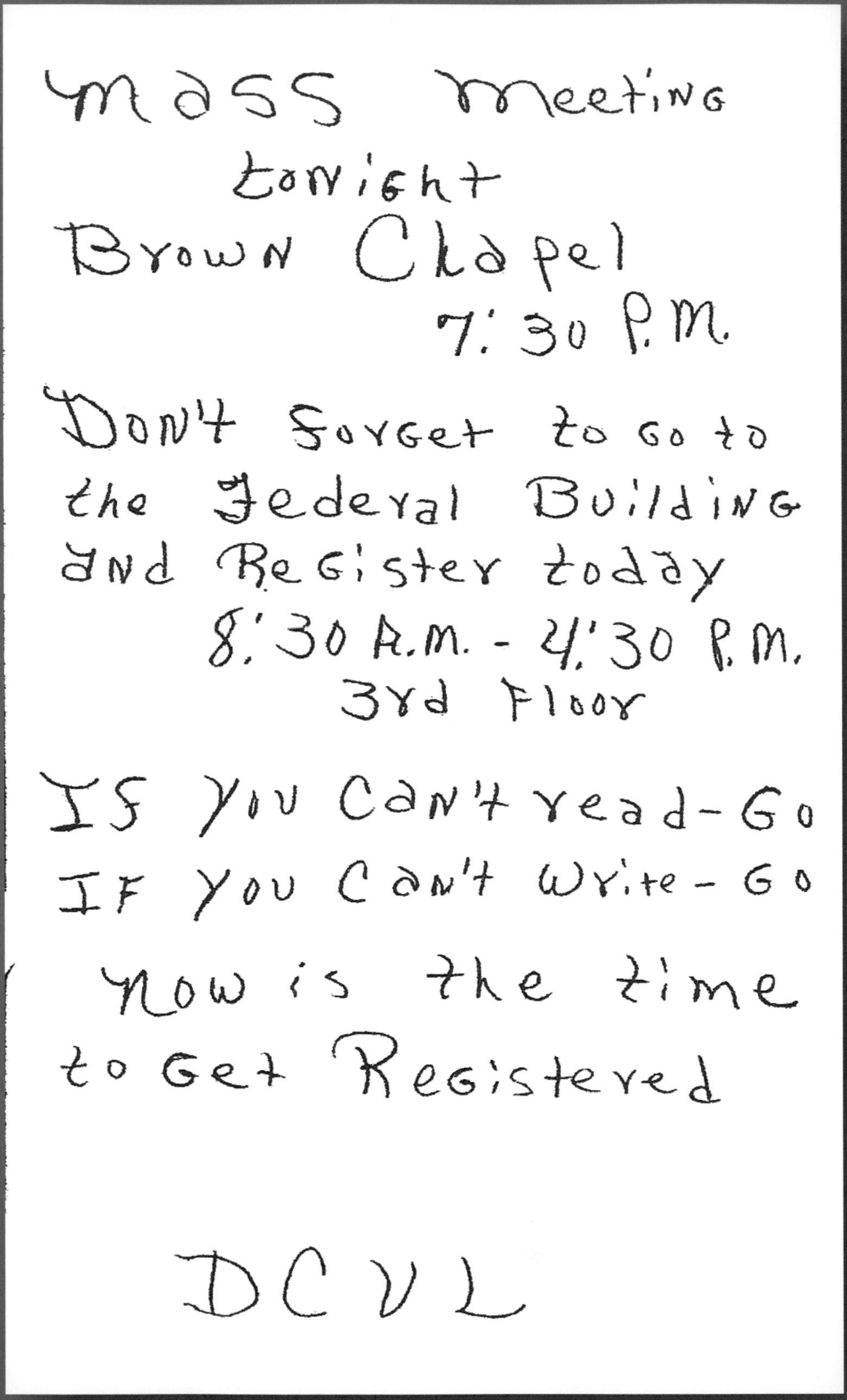

The new Voting Rights Act eliminated impediments to voting, and the Dallas County Voters League (DCVL) urged Selma residents to register.

Mass Meeting
tonight
Brown Chapel
7:30 P.M.

Don't forget to go to the Federal Building and Register today
8:30 A.M. - 4:30 P.M.
3rd Floor

IF you can't read - Go
IF you can't write - Go

now is the time to Get Registered

DCVL

On Sunday night, Jonathan visited Mount Carmel Baptist Church in Gordonsville, Lowndes County, for a mass meeting. "Everyone was wondering what was going to happen," a SNCC worker recalled, knowing that the preacher opposed the gathering. Despite the passing of the Voting Rights Act, the preacher was terrified that they'd all be shot at. But community members insisted on meeting.

Afraid to encourage blacks to vote if it meant they could lose their lives, their jobs, or their homes, the preacher meekly told the group that Heaven was the only place for peace and equality. Then he asked if anyone in the audience wanted to speak.

Jonathan strode to the platform and told the group where he was from, though it was obvious from his Yankee accent. "My freedom depends upon everyone having their freedom," he stated. The congregation was impressed. In five months, Jonathan had catapulted from an observer to a leader—front and center in the civil rights movement in central Alabama.

Jonathan's impact on the mass meeting was strong. People crowded around him and asked him to return in two weeks to speak at their next meeting. Jonathan promised that he would. First, he planned to attend the annual SCLC convention. King had chosen Birmingham, Alabama, as the site, and many meetings were scheduled to take place in the city's Sixteenth Street Baptist Church, where the four girls had died in a bombing two years earlier.

Before leaving for Birmingham, Jonathan was eager to put the Voting Rights Act to the test. He and the Sapersteins headed to Lowndes County on Tuesday, August 10, and visited several farms.

They had a long and productive day and worked up an appetite. But as civil rights activists, they would not be welcome at any Lowndes restaurant. They relied on the generosity of the farmers for meals.

Jonathan entered a field and asked a family he knew, "Can you fix us up some dinner?" They were invited into the family's tiny home, which had no running water or electricity. The Sapersteins wondered what they would eat.

"We entered the cabin and it was spotless—the table had been set," Rabbi Saperstein recalled. Freshly baked bread and several kinds of meat were on the table. Then the father of the house walked in.

"This is the second time white men have eaten at my table," he said with a smile, squinting at the fading light from the window, "but it is the first time a white lady has eaten at my table." Then he held up a card.

"I registered," the sixty-five-year-old man said. "For the first time, I feel that I'm a citizen."

No Back
Doors

RY & MARKET

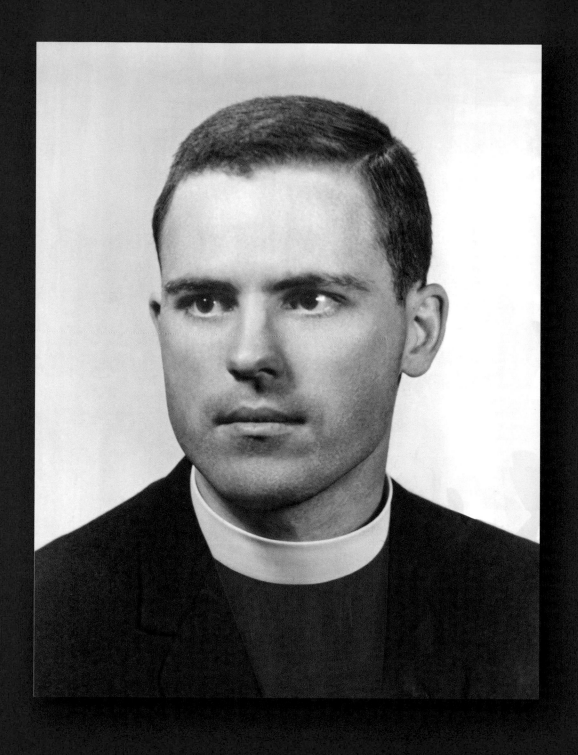

Jonathan eagerly listened to Martin Luther King speak at the SCLC convention. King had just flown from Washington, where he'd witnessed the signing of the Voting Rights Act. Now he urged workers to encourage blacks to vote, and he set a goal of a million new black voters for the fall's elections.

A thousand SCLC delegates and leaders of other civil rights groups attended the convention. SNCC's John Lewis pulled Stokely and Jonathan aside with a request: a white Roman Catholic priest from Chicago named Richard Morrisroe wanted to help in Lowndes County. Would they take him in?

After shaking Morrisroe's hand, Stokely and Jonathan hesitated. They were surprised to learn that Morrisroe was a priest, since he wasn't wearing a clerical collar. Morrisroe's experience as an activist was limited. He'd flown south after Bloody Sunday, but returned to his parish before the march to Montgomery because of a strep throat. Now he hoped to spend his vacation time learning about race relations in the South.

It had been five months since the march to Montgomery, and white northerners had stopped offering to roll up their sleeves in Alabama in significant numbers. The reason was murder. The deaths of Reverend Reeb and Viola Liuzzo had caused a wave of terror among white civil rights workers. In Lowndes County, Jonathan was the exception. John Lewis said Jonathan had become like blood to the county's black farmers. If Father Morrisroe wanted to work in Lowndes County for a week, Stokely and Jonathan would welcome him.

Chicago priest Richard Morrisroe came to Alabama to study race relations.

Jonathan joined Fort Deposit teenagers to protest poor treatment of blacks at this store and two others.

Morrisroe would replace Rabbi Saperstein, who'd returned to Long Island. When the SCLC convention ended, Jonathan and Morrisroe headed down the winding Highway 80 in Jonathan's Plymouth Fury.

Jonathan was eager to show Morrisroe around Lowndes County before the sun beat down on the farmers they'd be visiting. They would have to be persuasive. By now, the cotton plants stood shoulder high and ripe for picking. The sharecroppers whose job it was to harvest the cotton knew that if they stopped to register to vote, they'd risk being evicted from their homes or thrown off the farms as punishment. The farmers knew that even the presence of federal voting examiners could not prevent that from happening.

A YOUTH MOVEMENT

Despite the fears of many Lowndes County sharecroppers, advancements in the civil rights movement continued to inspire their children. Too young to vote but ready to take a stand, a few dozen black students decided to protest in the predominantly white town of Fort Deposit, where no blacks had ever dared to demonstrate. They chose the week's busiest shopping day—Saturday, August 14. Their plan was to picket three stores where blacks had been denied service, made to enter through back doors, or charged higher prices than whites: the Community Grill, Waters Dry Goods, and Ralph McGough's grocery store.

"Everybody was afraid because it was a white folks' town," said Geraldine Logan, a Fort Deposit teenager then. "They used to beat up black people and hang them on top of Skull Hill."

Word spread quickly. SNCC issued a warning to anyone planning to participate in the demonstration: "Klan is very active in area." SNCC chairman John Lewis contacted Governor Wallace and demanded police protection for the picketers, but the governor did nothing. Jonathan grew worried about potential violence toward the teenagers.

Journalist Bill Price also heard about the demonstration. A New York-based photographer for the *National Guardian* newspaper, Price was accustomed to dangerous situations. He'd flown air-rescue operations as a navy pilot in World War II, making emergency landings in the middle of the sea. Now in Alabama on a shoestring budget to cover the civil rights movement, Price didn't have a place to stay. SNCC said he could sleep on the Freedom House porch on Friday night, if he could find a spot. The porch was crowded with workers exhausted from their long day of canvassing, including Jonathan and Father Morrisroe.

As they rolled out their sleeping bags for padding against the worn plank floor, Price grilled Jonathan and Morrisroe about the movement and the attitudes of their churches. But while Price and Morrisroe chatted late into the evening, Jonathan stayed uncharacteristically quiet.

Jonathan swatted at mosquitoes as cicadas hummed in the steamy Alabama night. Tomorrow's demonstration in Fort Deposit could be bloody, but Jonathan knew that talking about the movement meant nothing without action. The young blacks in Fort Deposit were tired of talk. In a few hours those teenagers would be taking a major stand for the first time in their lives and he'd be there with them.

After midnight, someone asked for a ride back to Selma, so Jonathan made the trip and caught a few hours of sleep at the Wests'. On Saturday, August 14—the day of the picket—Jonathan woke up early to bathe and shave. Pulling on khaki pants, he laced up the hiking boots he'd worn during the march to Montgomery, adjusted his clerical collar, and slipped a cross into his pocket. Then he drove to Fort Deposit. Along the way he picked up as many SNCC workers and teenagers as he could cram into the car.

Older black residents also went to Fort Deposit that Saturday, not to picket, but to register to vote at the post office. With federal examiners now in charge, they could finally register without impediments. Waiting in line under the blazing sun, they hoped the presence of FBI observers might keep the young protesters safe.

With his camera around his neck, Bill Price made his way through the Saturday morning heat to Fort Deposit. He wanted to arrive before the Freedom House group and stake out a vantage point to cover the history-making demonstration.

Price wasn't the only journalist on the scene. By nine o'clock, David Gordon, a reporter with the *Southern Courier* newspaper, sat nervously in his car, watching a group of angry whites haul guns and clubs from the trunks of their vehicles. "The town looked like it was getting ready for a war," he wrote.

The white group gathered at Golson Motors, the car dealership owned by Lowndes County voting registrar Carl Golson. Golson was incensed that federal examiners were registering blacks at the post office down the street. News of the impending picketing sent him into a rage.

The white group looked suspiciously at David Gordon's car, but Gordon focused on another crowd gathering at a

church two blocks away: Jonathan had stepped out of his Plymouth Fury and chatted with Morrisroe, Ruby Sales, and some young SNCC workers and Fort Deposit teenagers.

Unaware of the threatening crowd, Jonathan and about twenty-five others gathered under a tree. Gordon warned them about the looming trouble from the white group at Golson Motors, which had grown and now included men with broken bottles, garbage can lids, and baseball bats.

The FBI agents cautioned that there would be nothing they could do if there was violence. "They were sure that someone would get killed if we carried on with the picket," a SNCC worker recalled.

PENT-UP ANGER

If they went through with the picket, would the Fort Deposit teenagers be able to remain nonviolent while being beaten by the Golson crowd and likely arrested by police? Years of bottled-up anger made for heated conversation. Stokely arrived and urged the group not to demonstrate if they couldn't do it peacefully.

Sitting on the church lawn with the others, Ruby Sales was nervous. She hoped there wouldn't be a picket but was ready to be part of it if that's what the young demonstrators wanted. "As frightened as I was—and I was frightened," she said, "I felt that it would be a supreme irony if we stopped them from picketing when we had been demonstrating all year."

Stokely had no intention of picketing. He planned to stay out of jail and keep working in the county. So did Jonathan, who expected to observe and take pictures in case there were arrests.

Police officers waited in anticipation of trouble on the morning of the Fort Deposit protest. One officer told photographer Bill Price, "There's a lot of tension here and I advise you to pack your things and get on out of here."

But "there weren't that many people in it," David Gordon observed, so Jonathan moved forward to "prop up the courage of the people and the local kids for whom this was their first demonstration." There weren't hundreds of picketers as there had been in Camden, and Jonathan wasn't going to stand around and watch these few, brave teenagers being beaten by white adults wielding baseball bats.

There was no question that Jimmy Rogers would participate. A wiry Tuskegee student with a calming demeanor, Rogers had spent four years in the air force. Brooklyn born, he'd never seen anything like the discrimination in Fort Deposit. "You could feel the hatred more there," Rogers explained. "That's where mostly the real hardcore Klan element was." He'd put his studies on hold and been assigned by SNCC to the Fort Deposit area. Rogers had strong reservations about whether the teenage protesters could be kept safe, but he agreed to lead the demonstration.

As the crowd of angry whites pressed closer with crude weapons, the young picketers knew they had to take a stand. Stokely told the picketers to discard anything that could be considered a weapon, such as pocket knives or nail files. "But they didn't have anything in their pockets," Rogers said.

Gathering their homemade signs, Rogers and the picketers decided it was time to move. They broke into three groups and headed downtown. "All of a sudden, there's people getting in line and started to march," said Price, who rushed to steady the camera around his neck. "There were these great constitutional principles enshrined in this sort of straggly little march."

The teenagers led Jonathan down a side street toward the flat stretch of one-story businesses. Jonathan smiled and joked to put the picketers at ease. Reaching the front of one of the stores, they marched in a circle, carrying signs that read EQUAL TREATMENT FOR ALL and NO BACK DOORS.

Astonished by what was happening, shoppers—blacks on one side of the street, whites on the other—gawked at the marchers. The group of white men with weapons approached. "I remember looking across the street and seeing a lot of white people with bats," picketer Geraldine Logan said.

But before the men could reach them, Jonathan's group was confronted by police. "What the hell are you doing here?" an officer yelled at him.

"Exercising our constitutional right to picket," Jonathan calmly replied.

"You don't have any rights in Fort Deposit," the officer told him. He arrested Jonathan and his group. The same thing happened to the other demonstrators.

"Groups of whites gathered in large numbers with shotguns, clubs, and nightsticks," one picketer remembered. He heard a loud voice yell, "Put them niggers in jail for disturbing the peace and parading without a permit."

Police arrest Fort Deposit teenagers after officers halted the peaceful demonstration.

LIKE GARBAGE

The group had protested peacefully. They were searched for weapons and led over the railroad tracks to the Fort Deposit jail: a two-room shack with bars that could barely fit all the picketers.

Stokely avoided the demonstration but was arrested when the car he hopped into bumped into one filled with angry whites. Now Stokely was locked in the crowded jail, too. But the Fort Deposit stay was temporary.

"The next thing I knew, we were being herded onto this garbage truck," Ruby said.

The dump truck was too crowded for anyone to sit down. Jonathan huddled close to the others to avoid the reeking garbage stuck to the sides. As they pulled away from the Fort Deposit jail and spotted the fearful faces of the black crowd watching them leave, Jonathan smiled and waved to calm their fears. But where was the truck taking them? He had no idea.

"We were singing freedom songs and saying, 'We're so glad we got on this garbage truck,'" Ruby recalled, "'cause those white men were getting ready to kill us."

Still sitting in his car, David Gordon wasn't so lucky. Carl Golson smashed the windshield with a club, leaving a trapped Gordon bloody from the spray of broken glass.

The garbage truck picked up speed along the bumpy, sixteen-mile trek with a police car close behind it, making it difficult for reporters to follow. Bill Price tried to keep up, pushing his rented car past seventy miles an hour before they reached their destination, the Lowndes County jail in Hayneville.

As the truck pulled into the driveway to the back entrance, Price rushed to the front, hoping to catch photos of the prisoners and information on why they'd been hauled to the Hayneville jail. A county official pointed to Price's camera, then pulled out a pistol. "If you value your property, you'll get out of here right now," warned the official. Price demanded to see identification. Enraged, the man showed him a card. It said: Jack Golson. CORONER. LOWNDES COUNTY. Jack Golson was registrar Carl Golson's brother.

Reminding Jack Golson about freedom of the press only angered him more. "It's you people down here excitin' all this that's causing all the trouble," Golson yelled, pressing a billy club against Price's head. But as more journalists arrived, Golson backed down. Price saw that the picketers didn't have that kind of advantage, though.

Whisked into the jail while the journalists were left behind, Jonathan and the group were soon out of sight of Price's camera.

Protesters arrive at the Hayneville jail in a garbage truck after being arrested in Fort Deposit. Stokely Carmichael is sitting in the lower right side of the truck.

Jailed

The Lowndes County jail in Hayneville

Jonathan and the other picketers had been slapped with trumped-up charges of parading without a permit and disturbing the peace. Since Stokely Carmichael hadn't picketed, his charges were reckless driving and leaving the scene of an accident.

Still wearing his seminarian collar, Jonathan gave his name to the jailers. They assumed he was lying and wrote down his last name as "Vaniels," stating that he used "Daniels" as an alias.

The group lined up against the white-tiled walls and waited for the jailers to figure out what to do with them. Unprepared for such a large group, the jailers led them into a holding area that doubled as the kitchen. As soon as the door was locked, the teenagers started venting.

The teens were angry for being thrown in jail after resisting the urge to use their fists during the Fort Deposit confrontation. Some of the young people asked, Why hadn't we fought back? What had nonviolence achieved? A trip to jail. Next time, some of them said, they *would* fight back.

Jonathan was frustrated, too, but a night in jail seemed better than the certain beatings they would have received in Fort Deposit.

A radio in the jail blared news of an ongoing riot in the Los Angeles neighborhood of Watts. For a third day, rioters cut a swath of violence through the African American neighborhood in California, burning cars and looting stores. It was also a revolt against police brutality, inadequate

Jonathan enters the Lowndes County jail on August 14, 1965.

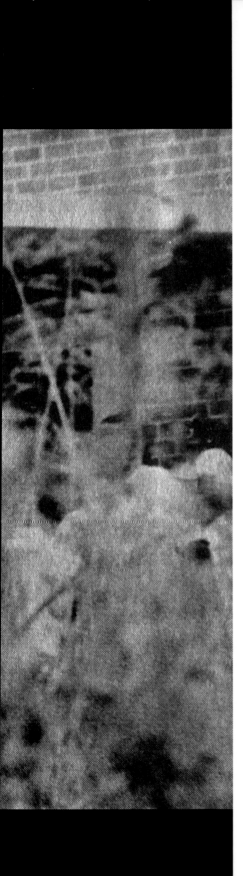

housing, and underfunded schools. Knowing that other blacks in the country were taking a stand—however extreme—struck a chord with some of the jailed picketers in Hayneville.

"We heard about the rebellion going on in Watts," said Gloria Larry, "which gave us some spirit."

But what was also occurring in Watts was murder. "A rioter with a Molotov cocktail in his hands is not fighting for civil rights," President Johnson declared, "any more than a Klansman with a sheet on his back and a mask on his face."

Jonathan fiercely opposed violence, too. Even if demonstrating peacefully in Fort Deposit had backfired, he reasoned, it was the only way he could live. "I am convinced that in the long run the 'strategy of love' is the only one that will bring real health and reconciliation into this mess," he'd told a friend. "Yet I sure understand when Negroes get impatient with 'nonviolence.' 'How long, O Lord, how long?'"

The jailers separated the male and female prisoners and herded the men upstairs to the second-floor cells. They threw Jonathan in the first and smallest cell with Stokely and another SNCC worker. Father Morrisroe was held with Jimmy Rogers and six other picketers. The Hayneville jail was segregated, but the handlers obviously didn't bother adhering to their own rule.

"UNBELIEVABLY FOUL"

Like most of the prisoners, Jonathan had never been jailed before. He'd racked up a few speeding tickets, but that's about it. What he saw shocked him. The county jail was filthy.

"The place was fetid," said Stokely, who'd been locked in other jails many times. "Unbelievably foul, even for a southern jail."

Each cell had an overflowing toilet that didn't flush. Being hauled there in a dump truck used to transport trash was disgusting, but this was much worse.

Jonathan's view was of a narrow, cement corridor. Across from his cell was a window too thick to see anything through except daylight and darkness. It was covered with a metal grate.

Jonathan eyed the toilets spilling waste onto the floor. He soon realized they had another problem—where to sleep. With more people than the number of steel beds in the cells, some would have to sleep on the floor.

Downstairs, the women didn't have it any better. Gloria Larry shared a cell with Lowndes County nineteen-year-olds Joyce Bailey and Geraldine Logan. Bailey worried that she would lose her job at the Fort Deposit pajama factory. The three talked nervously about being separated from the protection of their friends upstairs. Hecklers yelled nasty threats at them through the jail window, a six-inch square of glass near the ceiling of their cell. But they soon put their own fears aside to worry about the fourth cellmate, seventeen-year-old Ruby Sales. In the sweltering heat of the county jail, her health took a drastic turn. Burning from the pain of an ulcer attack, Ruby pleaded to see a doctor. The deputy refused. "Stop all that noise, or you'll have something to scream about!" he warned.

Ruby's biggest concern wasn't a painful ulcer but the consequences of being a minor with a jail record. She'd told the jailers that she was twenty.

"There was a terrible fear that it was going to be discovered that I was a minor," Ruby said, explaining why she lied about her age. "If you were a minor demonstrator you

	Age 50	C. H.	
	Height	Wt.	
No.	Nat'l W	Comp.	
Henry W. Vickery	Sex M	C. E.	
	Age 47	C. H.	
	Height	Wt.	
No.	Nat'l W	Comp.	
Jonathan Vaniels	Sex M	C. E.	
alias Daniels	Age 26	C. H.	
	Height	Wt.	
No.	Nat'l B	Comp.	
Willie Vaughn	Sex M	C. E.	
	Age 21	C. H.	
	Height	Wt.	
No.	Nat'l N	Comp.	
Robert James Virgen	Sex M	C. E.	
	Age 24	C. H.	
	Height 5''	Wt.	

Jailers recorded Jonathan's name as "Jonathan Vaniels" in the prisoner list. Intent on portraying Jonathan as dishonorable, officials insisted that "Daniels" was an alias.

would be taken away from your parents and they would be charged, because you were a delinquent, and you were a ward of the state." Ruby could be sent to reform school.

Upstairs, Sheriff Frank Ryals grew irritated. The prisoners had barely touched their meal of soggy beans.

"The food is vile," Jonathan wrote, sliding his paper plate outside his cell with the others. Big mistake. If the prisoners wouldn't eat the food, the sheriff had a solution. "If you won't eat it, I won't clean it up," he told them, leaving the mushy food to rot in front of the cells.

Word spread that the picketers were in jail. Frantic to know when they'd be released, the SNCC dispatcher in Atlanta kept calling the Lowndes County sheriff's office. But she was told that only the Fort Deposit mayor could give that information and that he was out of town, which was a lie.

By nightfall, anxious parents came to see their kids, hoping to bail them out of jail. When they heard that the cash bond for release was one hundred dollars per prisoner, they were shocked. Many of the parents earned just two dollars a day as sharecroppers, so that was an impossible sum. The best they could do was bring books to the prisoners to pass the time. Bail money would have to be raised by SNCC or ESCRU.

Friends handed the prisoners several books with themes of social consciousness, including the autobiography of Frederick Douglass and a novel with the provocative title *The Fanatics*. Jonathan's visitors would soon regret giving him *The Fanatics*. Forty-five days later, at the county courthouse, which was two blocks from the jail, attorneys would use that book against Jonathan's character—accusing him of being a fanatic himself—in a sensational trial that would shock the world.

HIGH FEAR

Concerned about the safety of the women downstairs, Jonathan convinced the jail's cook to pass notes to them. "It was a terrifying experience," and Jonathan's notes "meant a lot," Ruby said. "They were first of all sarcastic, sometimes joking, but never, 'Oh, woe unto us.' He was always trying to keep the spirit high."

Two cells over from Jonathan, sweat poured down Father Morrisroe's face as he jotted notes in a journal he'd borrowed from a cellmate. Jailed within forty-eight hours of arriving in Lowndes County, Morrisroe was in no mood to talk. He was frustrated with wasting his time in jail.

Sensing the fluctuating moods of his fellow prisoners, Jonathan had a note passed from cell to cell on Sunday morning. "We are having service at 11:00," he wrote. "I wish you could join us to sing and pray together."

Conducting the service, Jonathan did what had come naturally ever since he was a seven-year-old in the church choir. He sang.

We shall overcome . . . We shall overcome some day.

The men on the second floor joined in, then Ruby and the other women downstairs. The singing continued throughout the week. "We drove them nuts because we kept singing our freedom songs day and night," Jimmy Rogers said.

The triumphant voices of the integrated group could be heard in homes near the jail, where white residents watched the deadly rioting in Watts unfold on their television sets. They learned of other race riots in Chicago and protests in Springfield, Massachusetts. The singing a few streets away in the county jail reminded them of the tension in Hayneville, which angered and terrified them.

"Fever is at a high pitch," said a Hayneville resident, who felt they were being "pushed up in a corner and stepped on."

In the minds of segregationists, what was happening in Hayneville was the same as in Watts. It had been a dramatic week in Lowndes County. Blacks had stood up for their rights and picketed for the first time. They stood in line at the Fort Deposit post office in large numbers and succeeded in registering to vote under the protection of a group segregationists couldn't stop—the federal registrars. Jonathan had participated in all of it. Now he was singing "We Shall Overcome" with civil rights workers in the county jail.

A Lowndes County official complained that Jonathan and the other jailed civil rights workers screamed and hollered and made "so much noise at night that people in the community couldn't sleep." With the walls of their segregated world crumbling before their eyes, local whites still hoped they could stop it. State highway engineer and special deputy Tom Coleman was certainly going to try.

Coleman, who lived near the jail, believed that Jonathan was "antagonizing things" and "promoting trouble." He'd told a reporter that blacks in Lowndes County were treated well and they'd only cause trouble if outsiders stirred them up. There would be no Watts-type riot in Hayneville if Coleman could help it. So when Sheriff Ryals asked him to pick up riot gear for the county police department, Coleman was more than willing to do it.

NO RELEASE

When their court hearing was set for Saturday, August 21—seven days after the arrests—it became clear to Jonathan that the jail time would stretch well beyond one night. He and the others agreed on a pact: they would leave the jail only as a group, not individually.

Jonathan hadn't been allowed to call his mother, and he knew she'd be worried. So he asked the jailers for a pen and some paper, hoping the note would arrive in time for her birthday on Friday. They handed him a pencil, barely an inch long.

Dearest Mum, Jonathan scribbled,

An eminently peculiar birthday card but . . . I have been in jail. . . . We aren't allowed to bathe (whew!), but otherwise we are okay.

He wrote that he was fine, but in reality Jonathan and the others felt weak from hunger and the heat. They were also dehydrated. The tap water had been shut off, and the prisoners weren't allowed to leave their jail cells. With no air conditioning to provide relief from the heat, they pleaded for water. But they drank as little as necessary out of fear that the jailers would poison it.

No one was more upset about his child being in jail than Robert Logan, Geraldine's father. After visiting her, the quiet-mannered farmer couldn't sleep, pacing the living room floor in the house where he'd once nearly been killed by a carload of angry whites. He'd accepted his wife Sarah's quest for civil rights and quietly watched as she lost her teaching job because of it. Hearing about the rioting in Watts with twenty-one people already dead was too much to handle. He drove to the jail and bailed Geraldine out.

"I had to leave the rest of them, and I really didn't want to go," Geraldine recalled, feeling guilty for breaking the pact. "I wrote Jonathan a note on a paper towel that I was leaving. He'd driven me to Fort Deposit to picket. I wanted him to know that I didn't need a ride back home."

Jonathan wrote back, agreeing that it was best for Geraldine to leave. He promised that he'd see her soon.

The pact continued to unravel. Next to leave were Jonathan's two cellmates—including Stokely Carmichael, who was bailed out on Wednesday, August 18. It was agreed that as the Lowndes County field secretary of SNCC, Stokely would be more useful out of jail. He promised to come up with bail money for Jonathan and the rest of the group before their court date on Saturday.

Later on Wednesday, two ESCRU representatives— Reverend Henri Stines and Reverend Francis Walter—drove from Birmingham with the intention of bailing Jonathan out. On the way, Stines, who was black, was handed a speeding ticket for driving fifteen miles an hour in Selma. He and Walter were interrogated and released.

"FISH IN A BARREL"

As the two priests walked up the stairs at the Hayneville jail, the stench of rotting food and the unsanitary conditions were hard to swallow. But it was the easy access to the cells that alarmed the priests. "Anybody could have walked in that jail and shot 'em up," Stines said.

"It was just like fish in a barrel," said Walter, astonished that there were no guards around.

Jonathan's attitude surprised Reverend Walter even more than the despicable jail conditions. While the priests were met with a few greetings of "Hey, man!" most of the prisoners were quiet and withdrawn. Jonathan was the opposite. Smiling at the visiting priests, he stretched his arm through the cell bars to shake hands.

"He was acting like he was the cheerleader and it was his job to keep people encouraged and laughing," Walter said. He'd never met Jonathan, and he immediately didn't like him. "Because I misunderstood him," Walter admitted, "and I was scared."

It wasn't just the jail that frightened Walter. He was shocked that Jonathan wore a clerical collar and he believed that it made him a marked man. Walter refused to wear one unless he was safe inside a church.

The priests told Jonathan that they'd come to bail him out.

"Are you bailing all of us out?" Jonathan asked.

Stines shook his head. They'd only been able to raise enough money for Jonathan.

"Oh, no, no," Jonathan told them, rejecting the offer. "We are all bailed out or nobody is bailed out."

Stines couldn't believe it. "He absolutely refused to allow me to get him out," he said. "He would not feel good about it, leaving his brothers in jail."

Jonathan's refusal to leave angered Reverend Walter even more. "I felt like he didn't know, that he was from the North [and] he didn't know how bad things were," Walter said.

Ruby, who'd learned through a note from Jonathan that Stokely had been bailed out, admired Jonathan for staying. "The whole time we were in jail, Jonathan showed a great deal of integrity," she later recalled. "He didn't leave."

EVENSONG

Alone in his cell on Thursday evening, Jonathan took the cross from his pocket, reached for his Bible, and waited for the sun to set. Tired, sweaty, and with a scruffy, six-day beard, he began singing the Magnificat—his favorite prayer at Evensong.

Other than Father Morrisroe and Gloria Larry, most of the group had never heard the evening vesper. Still, it kept their spirits up. "Jon to some of us came as a leader, a leader of songs, a leader at times of prayer," Morrisroe recalled.

Little did they know that by Evensong the following night, a tragedy would change their lives forever.

The narrow hallway outside Jonathan's cell

THE CASH STORE

DRINK Coca-Cola

IN BOTTL

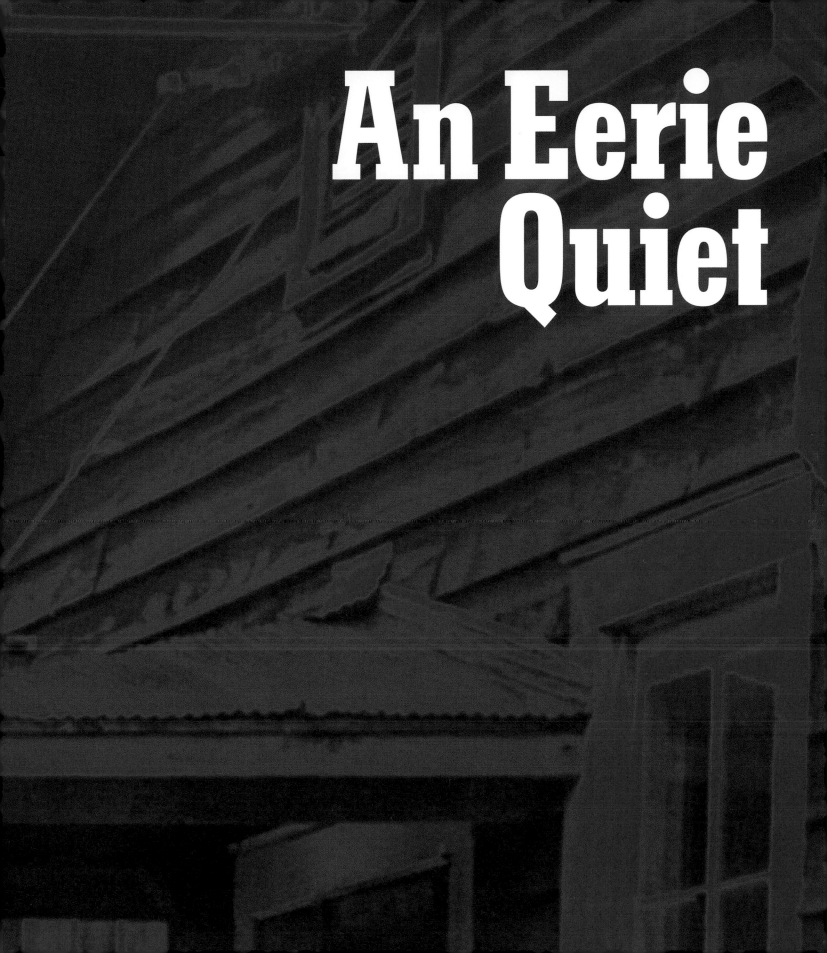

An Eerie Quiet

On Day 6, Jonathan woke up to the smell of rotting, fly-ridden food. Paper plates littered the hall just a few feet away, piled high with putrid beans. He ignored the stench and recited his morning prayers.

Temperatures soared into the 90s, and Jonathan steeled himself for another blistering day in jail. But crucial events were developing. A SNCC lawyer telephoned the Fort Deposit mayor to deliver a message. Certain that the group's reason for being jailed violated their civil rights, the lawyer had petitioned to have their cases moved to federal court instead of Saturday's planned hearing in Hayneville. But the lawyer still didn't have the money to bail the prisoners out.

News of the petition spread quickly through Lowndes County. Sometime after two o'clock, the prisoners were startled to hear footsteps and the rustling of a jailer's keys. The jailer unlocked the doors and told them they were free to go.

At first, "we were so happy to get out," said jailed SNCC worker Willie Vaughn. But why had they been released? Jonathan and Ruby grew suspicious and didn't want to leave. No one had to remind them about what happened the previous summer: three SNCC volunteers had been murdered in Mississippi immediately after they'd been released from jail.

"Who signed our bond?" Jimmy Rogers kept asking as they were hurried down the stairs to sign papers. He never received a response. Everything seemed so rushed. No phone calls allowed. Just sign the papers and go.

Jonathan had this bleak view from his cell for six days.

257

Having been cooped up in their cells for nearly 150 hours, the group squinted at the unfamiliar brightness. The daylight and steamy heat of the afternoon magnified their condition: they were sweaty, the men had beards, and everyone needed to shower. But at least they were free.

The relief of freedom quickly changed to alarm. No one was there to take them home. Not Stokely Carmichael, not family members, not Reverend Stines. It became obvious that they hadn't been bailed out by anyone they trusted. Otherwise, that person would be waiting for them outside the jail.

The streets were deserted. Hayneville residents had been warned of the prisoners' release and stayed indoors. "There was an eerie feeling," Ruby recalled.

Jonathan and his group sat on the prison's driveway. They agreed that the safest thing to do was to remain on jail property until someone they *did* know came to pick them up.

LOADED FOR TROUBLE

At the same time, in the county courthouse two blocks away, Tom Coleman finished a game of dominoes with his good friend Leon Crocker. Someone came in and whispered to Coleman. He grabbed his 12-gauge shotgun, gave the group a "signal," stepped into his black Chevrolet, and drove to Varner's Cash Store.

Deputies in a police cruiser idled nearby, then parked in front of Jonathan and the others with an order: get off jail property.

"This is government property," Willie Vaughn insisted. The lawmen didn't back down and demanded that the group leave.

Forced to walk away from the patch of land where they felt safe, the group didn't go far—just eighty yards past an old cotton gin to the street corner on Highway 97 and a bright red fire hydrant. Since they hadn't been allowed to make a call from the jail, Vaughn went looking for a telephone to ask for a ride. Jonathan and six others waited, but the rest of the group began the long walk home.

Hungry and thirsty, Jonathan scratched at the itchy growth of stubble under his seminarian collar. Half a block to the right, on the same side of the street, was the Cash Store with its tin roof and weather-beaten plank walls. Staring at the vapors of heat rising off the pavement, Ruby Sales and Joyce Bailey decided to buy a soft drink. "We'd been in jail, underfed, and we were thirsty," Ruby said.

Jonathan wanted a drink, too, but he didn't have any money. He asked Ruby if she had an extra dime for him. She did. "Will you all buy Richard [Morrisroe] one?" he asked. Ruby nodded. But "there was an ominous sense that filled the air and I became very nervous," she explained, "because it suddenly occurred to me that the street was clean of cars; there was literally no one around."

Brushing her fear aside, Ruby made her way to Varner's Cash Store followed by Jonathan, Morrisroe, and Bailey.

Jimmy Rogers stayed at the corner. "We could watch the door of the store," he said, "but see, they never really got in the store."

Tom Coleman waited for them. While Virginia Varner finished ringing out customers, Coleman reached for the shotgun he'd rested against the counter. Out back, the beauty shop—normally a beehive of activity on a Friday afternoon—was closed.

Unaware of Coleman's presence behind the screen door, Ruby stepped onto the concrete platform in front of the store. Jonathan was behind her.

"The store is closed," Coleman told them, appearing in the doorway. "If you don't get off of this goddamned property I'm gonna blow your damned brains out!" Coleman aimed his shotgun at Ruby and reached for the trigger.

"Next thing I knew someone had pulled me from behind," Ruby said. Jonathan pushed Ruby to the ground as Coleman fired. The force of the bullet threw Jonathan into the air, tearing a hole through his chest an inch wide. Clutching his side, Jonathan landed on the concrete platform. He was dead.

Grabbing Joyce Bailey's hand, Father Morrisroe turned and ran. But Coleman wasn't done shooting. His second shot hit Morrisroe in the back. The priest stumbled to the ground next to Coleman's car while Bailey sprinted behind the store and hid.

This is what it's like to be dead, Ruby thought, lying on the platform covered in Jonathan's blood. But when she heard the second shot, Ruby knew that she was alive. Hearing Coleman's footsteps beside her, she pretended that she *was* dead.

Coleman stood over Jonathan's body, then walked to Morrisroe. The other civil rights workers watched in horror from the corner.

"Ruby!" Joyce Bailey whispered.

Ruby managed to crawl down the steps and behind the store to Bailey. They sprinted across the street to Rogers and Vaughn.

Coleman waved his gun at them and they ducked for cover behind some bushes. Then Coleman got in his car, drove to the courthouse, and phoned authorities. "I just shot two preachers," he said. "You better get on down here."

Barely alive but still conscious of everything around him, Morrisroe moaned in agony, begging for water. Jimmy Rogers tried to help, but by then at least ten white men had gathered. They started making threats. "If you don't get away from here, you're gonna be lying there with them," they warned. So Rogers fled.

GRIEF TO RAGE

When an ambulance finally arrived half an hour later, Morrisroe clung to life but overheard the attendants talking. "This one's dead. This one's still moving," they mumbled. Hoisting Jonathan's body in first, they put Morrisroe on top. Then coroner Jack Golson drove to Baptist Hospital, twenty-five miles away in Montgomery.

A panic-stricken Ruby and the others had somehow found rides to the Freedom House. Willie Vaughn ran to make another phone call to the SNCC office in Selma, telling them the grim news.

SNCC chairman John Lewis was shocked by the murder. "Jon Daniels is dead in Alabama," he announced. "The ink was barely dry on the latest civil rights law. . . . What use is it to guarantee a man the right to vote, when there is no guarantee that he will not be murdered before he can get to the courthouse?"

When Stokely heard that Jonathan was dead, he let out a scream that sounded like a wounded animal. Then the tears began to flow. But his grief soon turned to rage as the murder of his close friend sunk in. Stokely drove to the

town square in Hayneville with a gun in his hand, ready to pull the trigger if anyone challenged him.

"I walked through the entire town," Stokely said, "almost daring them to come and shoot." No one did. "They thought I was crazy," he concluded. There were no traces of Jonathan's murder either. The Cash Store steps had been scrubbed clean of his blood and the crowd was gone.

In Montgomery, doctors operated on Morrisroe for eleven hours, saving his life. But where was Jonathan's body? SNCC dispatchers and ESCRU's Reverend Morris called every funeral home in the area. All of them denied having Jonathan, and time was critical. Both Morris and SNCC feared that the body would be tampered with to make it look as if there'd been a struggle or that Coleman had killed Jonathan in self-defense. Maybe they'd never find the body. Frantic, Morris called John Doar, an assistant attorney general of the United States, for help.

FIRST-DEGREE MURDER

In Keene, Connie Daniels tried to enjoy her birthday supper. Friends had taken her to a favorite restaurant and by chance, Bob Perry was dining there, too. When Connie spotted Jonathan's childhood friend, she rushed over to speak with him. "I'm worried about Jon," she admitted. "I know he's in jail, but I can't get any information from anyone down south. And Jon never forgets to call on my birthday."

Perry hadn't heard from Jonathan either, but on his drive home from the restaurant a report about Jonathan's death blared across his car radio. Pulling over, Perry turned and sped to Connie's home. But it would be several more hours before Jonathan's body would be found.

Varner's Cash Store in Hayneville, days after Jonathan's murder

John Doar finally located Jonathan's body at Montgomery's White Chapel Funeral Home. An autopsy had been performed, but the results were in the hands of the state police. They refused to give Doar any information.

At about the same time Jonathan was found, Lowndes County prosecutor Carlton Perdue stood in his office at the county courthouse. He couldn't stall any longer. After a five-hour meeting that included Sheriff Frank Ryals, Dallas County sheriff Jim Clark, and Tom Coleman's attorneys, Perdue charged Coleman with first-degree murder in the death of Jonathan Daniels.

"Tom Coleman has admitted the murder but has signed no confession," Perdue said.

Reporters kept pressing him for details about Jonathan's killing.

"They went down to this store to do some picketing and [Coleman] just let 'em have it," Perdue announced. "We're not going to pre-try the man," he added, pointing out that the person he'd just charged with murder was a friend of his.

But Perdue was willing to pre-try Coleman's victims. "If they'd been tending to their own business, like I tend to mine, they'd be living and enjoying themselves today," he said.

Sheriff Ryals insisted that Coleman "had a call to go down there to quiet a disturbance" and that Coleman "was acting in an official capacity as a peace officer." He later changed that story, believing it would help Coleman.

Coleman was escorted to the same jail that Jonathan had been released from seven hours earlier. But he wouldn't be there for long.

THE WORLD REACTS

The next morning, news of Jonathan's murder made headlines around the world. President Johnson demanded an investigation and ordered an FBI probe.

While visiting the decimated streets of Watts, Martin Luther King took time to write to Connie Daniels. He said that Jonathan's sacrifice was one of the most heroic actions he'd ever known. Expressing his grief, King wrote that Jonathan's death had fulfilled the meaning of a very promising life. He stressed that few people would accomplish as much in their lives as Jonathan had, even if they lived one hundred years.

Faced with another murder of a white civil rights worker in Lowndes County, the Alabama attorney general, Richmond Flowers, vowed that justice would prevail this time. "If this is murder, it will be prosecuted to the full extent of the law," he promised.

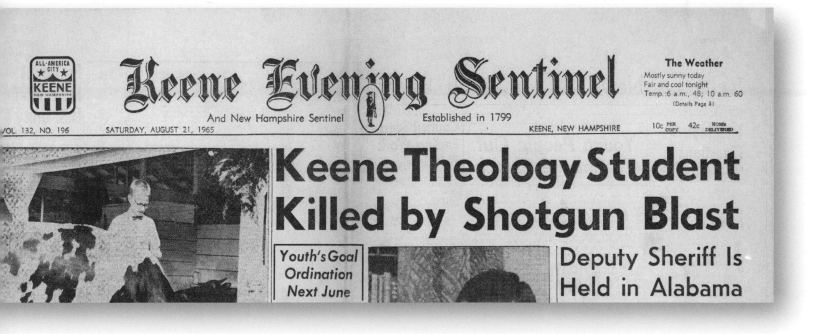

Slain Seminarian Knew Death Lurked in Alabama's Streets

United Press International

ATLANTA, Aug. 21—Jonathan Myrick Daniels, 26, a serious theology student from Keene, N. H., recently wrote of Alabama, "There are good men here, just as there are bad men."

Daniels, who had spent most of the past six months in Alabama as a civil rights worker, was shot to death on a Hayneville, Ala., street yesterday.

He was in Alabama as a representative of the Atlanta office of the Episcopal Society for Cultural and Racial Unity. The society described him as "studious," and "a man with a Christian commitment."

[In Keene, his mother, Mrs. Constance Daniels, told the Associated Press that her son went to Alabama to "do undramatic work like teaching in remedial schools run by the civil rights movement."

[She said he went to Lowndes County, Ala., "to aid the call for volunteers" issued last winter by the Rev. Martin Luther King. She was told of his death following a birthday party in her honor last night.]

Explains Work

Writing to the society, Daniels explained, "We are beginning to see, as we never saw before, that we are truly of the world, and yet ultimately not of it.

"We have activists who risk their lives to confront people with a challenge of freedom and a nation with its conscience. We have neutralists who cautiously seek to calm troubled waters. We have men of reconciliation who are willing to reflect upon the cost and pay for it."

A senior student at the Episcopal Theological Seminary in Cambridge, Mass., Daniels first came to Alabama in March. He became "concerned" over the civil rights work to be done and requested permission from Cambridge authorities to finish his school semester by correspondence. It was granted.

Working with whites and Negroes in Alabama's Black Belt became a moving experience for the dark-haired young man. He commented, "Sometimes we take to the streets, sometimes we yawn through interminable meetings. Sometimes we confront a posse, sometimes we hold a child."

Not Afraid

Officials of the society said Daniels never expressed fear for his life, "but he was aware of the dangers, and he took those precautions he could take."

Daniels recently attended the national Southern Christian Leadership Conference at Birmingham. While there, he commented to a friend about the possibility of being shot at by night-riders.

"I always keep my car windows up," Daniels said, "at least that would give a little protection."

Jonathan's slaying drew headlines in newspapers throughout the nation.

Rights Helper Slain, Priest Is Shot in Ala.

Hayneville, Ala., Aug. 20 (Special)—A white civil rights worker studying for the ministry was shot dead on a Hayneville street today. The rights worker, John Daniel, collapsed and died near the court house where a white Ku Klux Klansman stood trial in May for the nightrider slaying of another rights worker, Mrs. Viola Liuzzo.

A Catholic priest was critically wounded in today's shooting.

"Two civil rights workers have been shot on the street here, and that's all we can say," he added.

"From New Haven"

Deputy Sheriff Joe Jackson identified Daniel as an Episcopal seminary student from New Haven, Conn.

(Neither the Yale University Divinity School nor the Episcopal Berkeley Divinity School in New Haven said it had a student by that name. One source identified Daniel as connected with the Episcopal Society for Racial and Cultural Unity. His mother, the source said, was from Keene, N.H.)

The wounded priest was identified as the Rev. Richard Morrisroe, 26, assistant pastor of St. Columbus Church in Chicago. He was taken first to St. Jude's Hos-

(Associated Press Wirefoto)
President Johnson speaking on White House lawn.

(NEWS Map by Staff Artist)
John Daniel was killed (A) and Mrs. Viola Liuzzo was slain on route 80 (B), all in Lowndes County.

pital in Selma, then transferred to a Montgomery hospital.

Arrested in Picketing

Jackson said Daniel, Morrisroe and Ruby Sales, a Negro woman from Columbus, Ga., were arrested last week during civil rights picketing at nearby Fort Deposit.

They posted bond and were released today from the county jail here.

"We decided to walk up to the corner and wait until somebody came to pick us up. Nobody showed up, so we decided to go to the store," Miss Sales said.

The store was Varner's Store, a small grocery behind the county jail.

"The white man at the store told us the store was closed," Miss Sales said. "He had a shotgun and he said 'Get off my goddamned property before I blow your goddamned brains out, you bastards.' We hadn't even touched his steps.

Pushed Down, Heard Shot

"The next thing I knew I was on the ground. Somebody evidently pushed me to the ground. Next a shot rang out, and John had fallen down, and I was crawling along the ground."

She said Morrisroe "kept

hollering and moaning. It was awful.

"We looked back and this white guy who shot was standing over John's body with his gun like he was daring somebody to do something about it. It sounded like there were a lot of shots."

Hayneville is in Lowndes County, where Mrs. Liuzzo, a housewife from Detroit, was slain the night of March 25 at the end of the Selma-Montgomery civil rights march.

Crash Kills Klan Lawyer

It is about 40 miles south of Montgomery, which in turn is about 100 miles southwest of Tuscaloosa, where Ku Klux Klan attorney Matt H. Murphy was killed in an auto accident today.

It was Murphy who represented Collie Leroy Wilkins, the Klansman who was brought to trial for Mrs. Liuzzo's death. The trial ended in a hung jury and a new one was set for Sept. 27.

In the Hayneville jailhouse where Tom Coleman had spent the night, a deputy unlocked his cell. Family members had paid $12,500 to have him released on bond. Less than twenty-four hours after killing Jonathan Daniels, Coleman was free to go until a trial. If there was one.

"BRICK BY BRICK"

By Sunday, Stokely had calmed down. At a crowded mass meeting in Lowndes, he sounded like his old self and talked about forming a new political party. "We ain't going to shed a tear for Jon, 'cause Jon is going to live in this county," he said, rousing the audience. "We're going to build it back, brick by brick, until it's a fit place for human beings."

But news of Jonathan's death hit most white southerners differently. Some said he deserved to be killed for interfering, including members of St. Paul's Episcopal Church. That prompted Bishop Carpenter to issue a statement declaring that no matter how evil one's sin is, killing that person is wrong. The backhanded remark emphasized how much southern church-going segregationists despised Jonathan. And there would be no remembrance for him at St. Paul's. In fact, an ESCRU representative had been in Reverend Mathews's office listening to him complain about Jonathan when they'd received a call about his murder.

But ESCRU's John Morris had a more urgent problem: how to bring Jonathan back to Keene. Like the funeral homes, no commercial airline in the South wanted to be associated with the body of a slain civil rights worker. Morris grew desperate. Knowing that President Johnson had provided a presidential plane when Reverend Reeb was killed, Morris called the White House and asked for help.

An official interrupted the president's late-night snack to say that Morris was finding it impossible to return Jonathan's body to Keene "by commercial means, through either air or rail."

"The train won't carry it or the plane or what?" the president asked.

The official noted "the sensitivity of the matter," since Jonathan was a civil rights worker. "If he had been hit by a truck and killed, I assume that the mortuary in Montgomery would be making arrangements," he explained. Johnson instructed the official to call the airlines directly, "and let me know later."

Reverend Morris waited hours for an answer from the White House, then made a decision. He asked a friend who was a pilot and owned a small airplane to fly him and Jonathan's body to New Hampshire on Sunday night.

Holding the bag with Jonathan's body on his lap, Morris arrived in Keene just after midnight. "It's hard to get out of my mind and thought and feeling how it was to carry Jon's body to the plane," Morris said.

Jonathan was the first ESCRU worker to be killed, and his death confirmed a fear Morris had kept to himself since founding the organization six years earlier. He'd known the risks were great, but that the progress would be great, too. Jonathan had accepted that, and it had cost him

Pallbearers lift Jonathan's casket into a hearse after his funeral service at St. James Episcopal Church. The pallbearers included his high school friends Carlton Russell and Gene Felch.

Saying
Goodbye

A grieving Connie Daniels looks lovingly at a photo of her son the day before his funeral.

Stokely had spoken brave words after Jonathan's death, but he felt pain inside. Too stricken with grief to drive north alone for Jonathan's funeral, he asked his mother, who lived in the Bronx, to take him.

"I had never seen my son like that. Silent, grim, like a heavy, heavy weight was pressing on him," Stokely's mother recalled. "That entire trip I don't think he said two sentences. He didn't even play the radio. . . . I do think that this was the hardest thing my son ever had to do in the movement."

On Tuesday, August 24, more than four hundred mourners filled St. James Episcopal Church in Keene for Jonathan's funeral—the same gray stone church where he'd been confirmed as an Episcopalian only eight years earlier.

Before leaving for the church, a tearful Connie Daniels received a telegram: "I grieve with you in the death of your son," wrote President Johnson. "We labor towards the day when the cause of brotherhood may prevail, and the violence that sometimes scars the face of America may be ended."

Friends and family members and SNCC workers from the South listened as one of Jonathan's ETS professors read a paper Jonathan had written about his time in Selma.

Alice West listened intently while gazing at Jonathan in his casket. "Stokely and the rest of us came and we stood there and we looked at him, he was just so peaceful," she said. "I had a good heart then because if I hadn't I would have had a heart attack. Just seeing him lying there, you know, such a good warm-hearted person had to get killed so violently."

EXECUTIVE

ME1-3/D

Daniels, Jonathan

Morris, John B.

FILES

August 23, 1965

MRS. PHILIP DANIELS

67 Summer Keene Street

Keene, New Hampshire

I GRIEVE WITH YOU IN THE DEATH OF YOUR SON. WE LABOR TOWARDS THE DAY WHEN THE CAUSE OF BROTHERHOOD MAY PREVAIL, AND THE VIOLENCE THAT SOMETIMES SCARS THE FACE OF AMERICA MAY BE ENDED. MAY GOD COMFORT:YOU AND STRENGTHEN YOU IN THIS HOUR.

LYNDON B. JOHNSON

RECEIVED
AUG 24 1965
CENTRAL FILES

LBJ:rgm

In a telegram to Selma civil rights leaders, Martin Luther King Jr. commended Jonathan for his courage. King called Jonathan's actions "one of the most heroic Christian deeds of which I have heard in my entire ministry and career for civil rights."

WESTERN UNION
SENDING BLANK

| CALL LETTERS | GDC | CHARGE TO | SCLC | AUG 27 1965 |

Joint Memorial Committee
c/o Harold Middlebrooks
21 Franklin Street
Selma, Alabama

One of the most heroic Christian deeds of which I have heard in my entire ministry and career for civil rights was performed by Jonathan Daniels. I have recently learned that the Deputy Sheriff pointed his gun through a door at the two Negro girls who were walking in front of Jonathan. Jonathan pushed the girls to the ground and gave his life for them.

More   More

Send the above message, subject to the terms on back hereof, which are hereby agreed to

PLEASE TYPE OR WRITE PLAINLY WITHIN BORDER—DO NOT FOLD
1269—(R 4-55)

WESTERN UNION
SENDING BLANK

| CALL LETTERS | GDC | CHARGE TO | SCLC |

Certainly there are no incidents more beautiful in the annals of church history, and though we are grieved at this time, our grief should give way to a sense of Christian honor and nobility for this church and the movement gave to the world a true follower of our Lord and Savior Jesus Christ. Jonathan certainly had a promising life and it is still a tragedy that it was cut so short by this brutal and bestial deed. But the meaning of his life was so fulfilled in his death that few people in our time will know such fulfillment or meaning though they live to be a hundred.

Martin Luther King, Jr.

Send the above message, subject to the terms on back hereof, which are hereby agreed to

PLEASE TYPE OR WRITE PLAINLY WITHIN BORDER—DO NOT FOLD
1269—(R 4-55)

Stokely had been to seventeen funerals for murdered civil rights workers, but this one hit him hardest. "I meet a lot of white people who come down south every day," he said. "I meet very few who have the insight that Jon Daniels had. And I met only one that I liked very much."

Unwilling to leave the cemetery after Jonathan's family members and northern friends had gone, Stokely remained by Jonathan's grave and began to hum. As he joined hands with fellow SNCC worker Willie Vaughn, the hum gave way to a familiar song:

We shall overcome, Stokely cried out. *We shall live in peace . . . black and white together.*

WHEELS OF JUSTICE

Before returning to the South after the funeral, Ruby and the other SNCC workers who'd witnessed Jonathan's murder were anxious to tell their story on tape. Each could provide testimony against Coleman, and they were afraid they might be killed to prevent them from appearing at a trial. After the murder, they'd asked the FBI for protection, but the feds offered none. Assistant Attorney General John Doar annoyed Ruby by telling her that "the wheels of justice move slowly."

The witnesses agreed to be interviewed by an Episcopal official, who tape-recorded their statements about the deadly afternoon in Hayneville. They insisted that the murder had been planned. "We were set up," Ruby said, "and were let out of jail specifically for someone to be killed."

After making the recording, Ruby and the others went into hiding. They hoped for justice and planned to testify at Coleman's murder trial. But they'd have to wait until

"In dying, not only was Jonathan Daniels minding his own business, but he also was attending to His business."

—THE *KEENE EVENING SENTINEL*

September, when a grand jury would decide whether to proceed with a trial.

In the meantime, Stokely wasn't taking any chances in Lowndes County. He vowed that SNCC would return to its former policy and never allow another white civil rights worker in Bloody Lowndes.

Stokely Carmichael and other mourners join hands and sing "We Shall Overcome" at Jonathan's grave.

The Coleman Trial

Tom Coleman approaches the Lowndes County Courthouse on the first day of his trial.

On September 15, three weeks after Jonathan's funeral, Richmond Flowers waited nervously for a phone call from Lowndes County. A grand jury in Hayneville was hearing evidence on Tom Coleman's first-degree murder charge. Flowers knew that the world expected justice, but the Alabama attorney general wasn't optimistic.

Four civil rights workers had been murdered in Alabama in 1965, and no one had been punished for the crimes. There'd been no verdict in the trial of the Klan killing of Viola Liuzzo, and no one had been charged for the murders of Jimmie Lee Jackson and Reverend Reeb.

"Justice and law and order has completely broken down," Flowers declared. So when the grand jury decided to reduce the charge against Coleman from first-degree murder to manslaughter, Flowers was enraged. The new charge meant that if Coleman was found guilty of killing Jonathan, he could not be sentenced to more than ten years in prison. The maximum penalty for first-degree murder was death.

Flowers was also angry when he learned which two attorneys would lead the prosecution of Coleman. Lowndes County solicitor Carlton Perdue was a friend of Coleman's, and Arthur Gamble was the attorney who had failed to firmly present the prosecution's case in the Liuzzo trial. Could Perdue or Gamble be trusted to present incriminating evidence against Coleman? Flowers didn't think so.

His doubts were confirmed by damaging statements Perdue made to reporters about Jonathan and the other civil rights workers. Perdue claimed they'd plugged up the jail toilets themselves, and he refused to believe that Jonathan was a seminarian or Father Morrisroe a priest. With Perdue viewing Jonathan as an outside agitator, it became clear where the prosecutors stood: with the defendant, Tom Coleman.

Flowers instructed his staff to collect their files on the case. The attorney general's office was taking over the prosecution of Tom Coleman.

THE TRIAL BEGINS

On the morning of September 28, Ruby Sales shivered outside the giant pillars of the Lowndes County Courthouse, sharing a coat for cover with murder witnesses Joyce Bailey and Jimmy Rogers. But it was raining so hard that the group was soaked.

"We were all made to wait out in the rain like cattle," Ruby said of that day in Hayneville. Newly hired African American guards stood nearby in khaki uniforms, armed with pistols and clubs. They'd been told to keep the civil rights workers in line.

Having to wait outside was a frustrating reminder of what Jonathan died for and what Ruby and the group still did not have: equality. Even in a courthouse where their constitutional rights were supposed to be honored. The only witnesses allowed to stay in the courthouse were white. "The prosecution didn't fight for us to be in the witness room," Ruby explained.

Inside the crowded courtroom, ESCRU's John Morris sat on a wooden bench, wedged between friends of Tom Coleman, while a deputy's dog wandered around freely, getting pats from state troopers. But when an eighteen-year-old black man tried to sit on the "white" side, an angry state trooper told him, "Keep your black tail out." The throng of reporters from newspapers across the country reached for their notepads, stunned that the courtroom was still segregated.

Segregated courtrooms were illegal everywhere in the United States, ever since the Civil Rights Act was put into law in 1964. Lowndes County judge T. Werth Thagard chose to ignore it.

Tom Coleman was tried in this courtroom in the Lowndes County Courthouse. He sat at the table with the two chairs and the ashtray, ten feet from the witness stand.

The Lowndes County Courthouse was built by enslaved blacks before the Civil War, and in many ways, transactions inside the green-shuttered courtroom still stuck to the laws governing the South a hundred years before. Judge Thagard's practices of segregating the courtroom and keeping blacks out of the jury pool were both illegal, but he'd never been charged with violating the law, so he kept doing it. Of the sixty jurors who could have been selected for Coleman's trial, all were white men, including Tom Coleman. His name had been picked as a potential juror for his own trial!

Coleman's name was struck from the list by the district clerk in charge of jury selection. Her name was Kelly Coleman. She was Tom Coleman's cousin.

The state attorney general's office had no intention of trying Tom Coleman that day. Richmond Flowers instructed an assistant to push for a postponement. "I think the climate is so bad in Hayneville right now, in Lowndes County," the assistant told Thagard, "that it's impossible for the state to get a fair trial."

The judge denied the request. The assistant kept pressing, arguing that the state's key witness, Richard Morrisroe, needed more time to recover from his injuries but had promised to testify when doctors permitted. The attorney general was deeply concerned that most of the state's witnesses to be called by Gamble and Perdue were Coleman's friends, and urged to delay the trial.

"The motion is denied," Judge Thagard told him. The silver-haired judge bristled at anyone interfering with his territory, but what he did next was unheard of. He ordered the attorney general's lawyer off the case.

Spotting Arthur Gamble, Thagard asked him if he was ready to go to trial.

"Yes sir," Gamble replied. So Thagard put Gamble back in as the lead prosecutor. An all-white jury was quickly assembled, and Thagard ordered the trial to begin.

"DID YOU HEAR A SHOT?"

Tom Coleman walked calmly to the front of the courtroom, chewing a wad of gum. He'd been a free man since the morning after killing Jonathan on August 20. Coleman wore a dark suit, a cold stare, and the same glum expression reporters had become familiar with. But they wouldn't hear Coleman speak. He had no plans to testify. Coleman would observe his trial while sitting at a table a few feet from the juror's box. Inside that box sat twelve white men, all of them friends and neighbors of Tom Coleman, including the jury foreman. Like Coleman, the foreman was a highway engineer.

Coleman's lawyers would speak for him. His nephew, attorney Robert Coleman Black, would help defend his uncle. Leading the three-man defense team was state senator Vaughan Hill Robison.

A tall and wiry politician who rarely smiled, the sandy-haired Robison had fought hard to keep Montgomery buses segregated despite a Supreme Court ruling against it. He had a talent for flustering witnesses by peppering them with rapid-fire questions, then switching the subject.

"How does the defendant plead?" the judge asked Coleman's attorneys.

"Not guilty, your honor."

Now it was up to state prosecutors to prove that Coleman was guilty.

As songbirds flew in and out of the courtroom windows, the soft-spoken Arthur Gamble took the floor. He called the prosecution's first witness: deputy sheriff Joe Jackson. With his gray hair clipped into a crewcut, Jackson was part of Lowndes County's three-man law-enforcement team along with his brother Luck Jackson and Sheriff Ryals.

Gamble asked Jackson if Jonathan Daniels had been searched for weapons before his release from jail. The deputy said Jonathan was searched when he was arrested in Fort Deposit. Jackson also testified that he'd been in the squad car six days later, when his brother ordered Jonathan and the other civil rights workers off jail property.

"Specifically, on August 20th," Jackson was asked, "had you been expecting any trouble here in the county?"

"No, sir," Jackson replied.

Virginia Varner, the owner of the Cash Store, later echoed Jackson's testimony. Wearing a navy dress and black gloves, she sat stiffly on the witness stand.

"Now, Mrs. Varner, before Tom Coleman came down there, that afternoon, did you call him and request that he come?" Gamble asked.

"No. I did not," she said. So Coleman hadn't been called. Prosecutor Carlton Perdue had told reporters that Varner telephoned Coleman for help. Varner also testified that the Cash Store had never been closed, as Coleman claimed. Not before Coleman killed Jonathan or after.

"Did you hear a shot fired?" Gamble asked Varner.

"Yes, I did."

"What did you do when the shot was fired?"

"I was actually making change when the shot was fired," she told the courtroom, "and I continued—I just went on with the business."

As defense attorneys cross-examined Jackson and Varner, their stories took a different turn.

The defense portrayed Tom Coleman as helping the understaffed sheriff's office enforce the law in Lowndes County when he killed Jonathan. But according to the FBI, Sheriff Ryals had told them Coleman wasn't a deputy at all. Ryals said Coleman had been given what three hundred other white men in the county carried in their wallets: a special deputy card, which was really just a gun permit.

"Do you know whether or not Mr. Coleman went up to Montgomery to get some riot equipment that day?" the defense attorney asked Joe Jackson.

"Yes, to maintain peace and order," Jackson said.

"And to keep down violence?" the attorney prompted Jackson.

"Yes, sir," Jackson said.

The attorney followed a similar tactic with Virginia Varner, trying to show that there had been a threat of danger when Jonathan and the other prisoners were released from jail. "Now, Mrs. Varner, you knew that the civil rights workers had been released?" he asked her.

"That's correct."

"And, you had called your daughter and made the fact known to her and told her to lock the doors there, in the house, just shortly before this happened?" the attorney reminded her.

Varner acknowledged that she had.

Things didn't look good for the case against Coleman. The defense had reinforced the risk of danger in the minds of the male jurors. Law enforcers had called for riot gear in time for the release of Jonathan and the other civil rights workers. But if the released prisoners were such a threat, why hadn't the riot gear been used, and why had Coleman been playing dominoes at the time of the release? The prosecutors never asked those questions.

"ADDITIONAL FREIGHT"

If the state toxicologist's gruesome account of how Jonathan died couldn't help the case against Coleman, nothing would. Taking the stand, the toxicologist told how a blast from a 12-gauge shotgun at close range—about six feet—tore a jagged hole through Jonathan's chest "one and one-eighth inch in diameter." He held up the nine lead pellets that had destroyed Jonathan's major vessels and his liver, causing massive bleeding. Jonathan had bled to death.

Gamble asked if the toxicologist had the clothing Jonathan wore when he died. The toxicologist reached for Jonathan's blood-soaked shirt and clerical collar, hushing the courtroom.

The state crime lab had also run tests using Coleman's shotgun and the spent shells. Leon Crocker, Coleman's dominoes partner, had scooped the shells off the Cash Store's cement platform, took them home, and tossed them into a trash barrel, but they'd been recovered. Comparing the results with Coleman's empty hulls, the toxicologist found no room for doubt. They were an exact match.

"There was ample evidence to identify the markings on the two fired cartridges," he told the jury, "as having been fired in that particular gun."

Lowndes County clerk and stenographer Charles Higgins carries the 12-gauge shotgun that Tom Coleman used to kill Jonathan Daniels.

The defense couldn't deny that Jonathan had been killed by a blast from Coleman's shotgun. Or could they? Attorney Vaughan Robison cross-examined witnesses only if he'd found a tactic he could exploit. Robison quickly took the floor to question the toxicologist. Had he found a loophole? But what Robison did next surprised the courtroom. Instead of bombarding the toxicologist with specifics about the shooting, Robison politely asked if he had other items found on Jonathan Daniels to show the jury.

"Some additional freight," the toxicologist said.

"May I see the book, please?" Robison asked.

The toxicologist opened the lid of a plastic container and handed a book to Robison.

"*The Fanatics*, I believe it is?" Robison told the jurors. He held up the novel that visitors had given Jonathan to read while in jail. Robison slammed the book on the table. Then he asked the toxicologist about notes found by an officer from a prisoner signed "Love, Joyce" to "Jonathan Daniels."

Gamble, the prosecuting attorney, finally sprang into action.

"We object to that!" Gamble hollered. But it was too late. The defense had begun a new line of attack, at one point holding up the maroon underwear Jonathan wore when he was killed. The attorneys strongly implied that Jonathan hadn't been in Lowndes County for civil rights work or as an honorable representative of a church, but to have affairs with black women.

It was now clear who was really on trial. It wasn't Tom Coleman. It was the character of Jonathan Daniels.

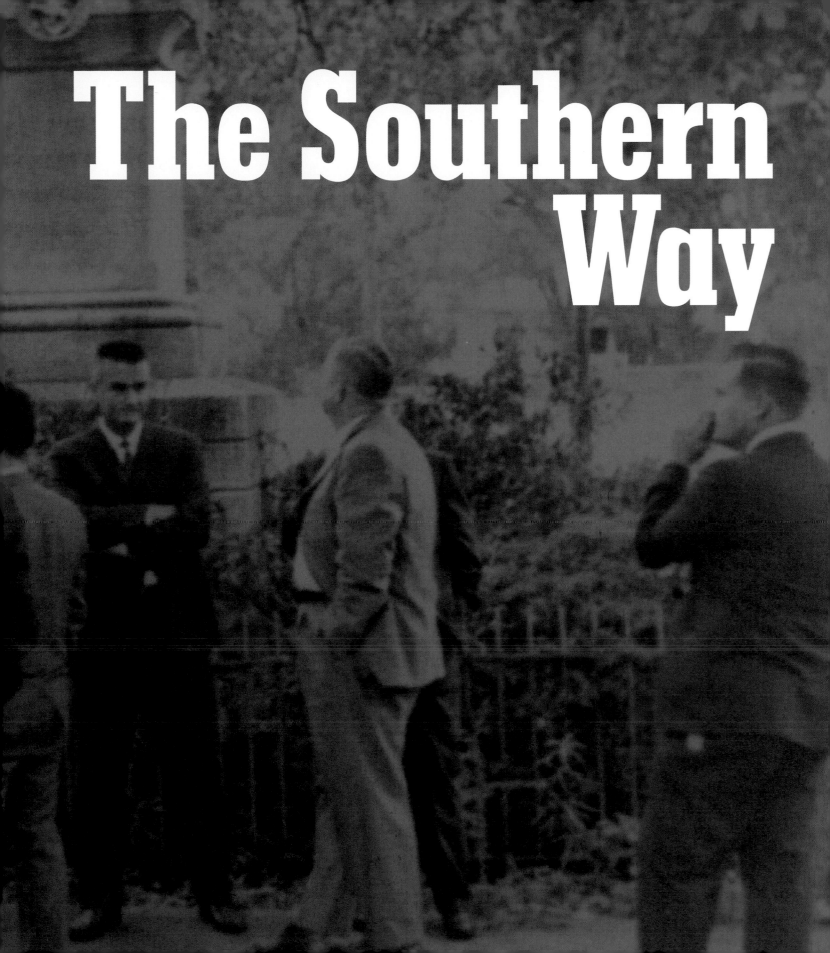

The Southern Way

Despite death threats, SNCC workers and Jonathan's friends walk to the courthouse to testify in Tom Coleman's trial. From left, Gloria Larry, Ruby Sales, Joyce Bailey, Jimmy Rogers, and Willie Vaughn.

At his home on Long Island, Rabbi Harold Saperstein was anxious for news of the trial. When he caught a glimpse of Tom Coleman walking into the Lowndes County Courthouse on TV, a chill ran through him. Saperstein believed Coleman was the same man who had stopped Jonathan's car in August on a remote county road. Coleman, Saperstein remembered, had looked inside the car and, spotting the rabbi and his wife, hesitated long enough for Jonathan to drive away. Now Saperstein worried that Coleman would get away with the killing of his friend.

In Hayneville, before the second day of the trial began, jurors gathered around the statue of a Confederate Civil War soldier, smoking and telling jokes.

Ruby Sales and Jimmy Rogers waited outside the courthouse, still hoping to testify, but angry that they hadn't been told if and when that would occur. Stokely Carmichael kept them company. He gave them "a pep talk because we were discouraged and pissed off about being in the rain," Ruby said. "He encouraged us that our testimony about Jon's murder was more important than whether we stood in the rain."

Rogers finally asked an official when he would testify. The man laughed and said, "Never!"

"We knew too much," Rogers recalled with disgust. "They weren't going to put us on the stand."

The witnesses called by prosecutors that day kept stepping around the killing. They testified that they'd seen Coleman carry the shotgun into the Cash Store. They even heard it fired. Twice. But no one admitted to seeing Coleman pull the trigger. Except Tom Coleman. He'd given an oral confession saying he killed Jonathan Daniels and gunned down Father Morrisroe. But that was written into a police report that was never read to the jury. In that report, Coleman made a claim that would dramatically change his role in the shootings. He said that when he told the group the store was closed, Jonathan asked, "Are you threatening me?" and that Jonathan and Morrisroe brandished weapons. Coleman said he killed Jonathan and shot Morrisroe because he feared for his own life.

The defense team admitted that they didn't have evidence that either Jonathan or Morrisroe was armed. "We can't show that a weapon was brought to them," they said. But that made no difference to their line of questioning. The attorneys spent the rest of the trial claiming that Coleman killed Jonathan in self-defense, and they used the prosecution's witnesses to try to prove it.

HEAVY DAMAGE

The prosecutors called as a key witness one of Coleman's closest friends—his dominoes partner, Leon Crocker. Crocker was familiar and comfortable in the Lowndes County courtroom. He was the bailiff—an officer of the court.

Adjusting his thick eyeglasses, Crocker testified that he was sitting on the bench in front of the Cash Store as Jonathan and the group—including "two nigger women"—walked to the store steps. He'd even heard the shotgun blast, but "I couldn't see the gun, or the man." Crocker's vision was clear enough to testify that Jonathan carried something in his right hand. "There was a bright shiny object that resembled a knife blade," Crocker said under oath.

"When, Mr. Crocker, did you see this shiny object that resembled a blade?" he was asked.

Crocker fidgeted. He'd been looking around the courtroom but quickly lowered his head and stared at his hands. "When I heard Daniels ask Tom, 'Are you threatening me?' I looked up," Crocker said, "and he had the knife in his hand."

This was precisely the kind of questionable but damaging testimony from a state witness that Richmond Flowers feared. He believed that Crocker had been told to say Jonathan was armed to help cover up a cold-blooded, premeditated murder.

"Did you see, Mr. Crocker, anything in Morrisroe's hand?" the defense asked.

"I took it to be a pistol," Crocker replied. "It was a round object that looked like a gun barrel, in his hand."

Reporters in the room who'd covered major trials across the country weren't buying it. They knew that if Jonathan or Morrisroe had been carrying weapons, they'd be on display in the courtroom as evidence, next to Coleman's shotgun.

ESCRU's Reverend Morris didn't believe the weapons story either. Fuming over such false and damaging testimony about Jonathan, Morris was convinced that the trial was a conspiracy and the prosecution was part of it. "The state made no effort to establish the fine character of this dedicated servant of Christ," Morris lamented.

Four black civil rights workers who'd witnessed the shooting were called to the stand. All denied that Jonathan or Morrisroe had weapons. "They didn't have anything," Joyce Bailey testified, clutching a blue raincoat.

Bailey was asked what she did when she heard the first shot. "I was running," she answered, nervously.

The courtroom erupted into laughter. Sipping from a glass bottle of Coca-Cola, the judge smiled.

Prosecutor Arthur Gamble later read aloud a written statement from Richard Morrisroe. "Daniels did not have a knife, gun, stick, or other weapon in his hand," Morrisroe wrote. "The only thing I had in my hand was a dime."

KEY TESTIMONY

It was finally time to bring in a key witness who'd been waiting outside.

"Ruby Sales!" an officer yelled from the courthouse window. "Come on up here."

Not "Miss" Ruby Sales. In 1965, it was common courtesy to use *Miss*, *Mr.*, or *Mrs.* before a person's name. But in this southern courtroom, the courtesy extended only to whites. Seventeen-year-old Ruby slowly made her way into the courthouse, taking deep breaths. She knew that the other female civil rights workers had been referred to as "hon" and asked to speak louder, or to tell the courtroom the exact address of where they lived.

"The people who testified took all kinds of risks with their lives," Ruby recalled. "When I walked up to testify, a white man in the courtroom pulled a knife on me and told me he'd cut my guts out."

If Ruby was afraid, she refused to show it. She glared at Coleman, who sat directly across from her less than ten feet away, smoking a cigarette.

"Tom Coleman came running out of the store with a gun—to the door of the store with a gun, and he told us that the store is closed," Ruby testified. "I didn't even have a chance to turn around, neither did Jon have a chance to turn around, and the next thing that I knew someone had pulled me from behind, and I stumbled to the side, and the next thing I knew I heard a shotgun blast."

Ruby's account of the killing rocked the courtroom. For the first time, a witness directly stated that Coleman was the aggressor in killing Jonathan and that Jonathan and the other civil rights workers were defenseless to stop him. This was the kind of eyewitness testimony Flowers had expected, but it made attorney Gamble uneasy. It didn't fit into his argument or the defense's—that Jonathan had threatened Coleman with words, a knife, or both.

"Jon immediately fell to the ground, and he didn't say not one single word through the entire occurrence—," Ruby said.

"Now, wait a minute," Gamble interrupted.

"I did not see a knife or pistol in either of the gentlemen's hands," Ruby insisted.

Vaughan Robison jumped up to cross-examine Ruby. "What kind of work were you all doing?" he demanded.

Ruby's answer made history. "We had been working in Lowndes County . . . to rid the racial barriers in this area, and that's—"

"That's the way that you all do it?" Robison interrupted.

Ruby ignored him "—our rights under the Constitution of the United States," she continued. "That's exactly what we were doing."

For the first time, the Lowndes County courtroom heard an African American woman testify that she was exercising her constitutional rights.

Incensed, Robison tried another tactic. "What did you all have on the picket signs down there, do you know?"

"We had 'Equal Treatment for All' and . . . 'No More Back Doors.'"

Robison changed the subject. "Did you write any letters while you were in jail?"

"Of course I wrote letters while I was in jail," Ruby replied.

"Who did you write those letters to?"

"I wrote letters to Reverend Jonathan Daniels, a personal friend of mine," Ruby stated.

The courtroom went wild. "Order in the court!" shouted bailiff Leon Crocker, back on duty after testifying. Ruby had made quite an impression. Yet for many whites in the audience who refused to admit that all races were equal, the last thing they wanted to believe was that whites and blacks could be friends.

"THAT KNIFE"

When order was restored, the defense team called their witnesses. One by one, friends and co-workers of Tom Coleman testified that they saw Jonathan and Morrisroe carrying weapons, or that they'd seen civil rights workers removing weapons from their bodies after the shootings.

The accounts strained belief. But it was what most spectators wanted to hear. Some whispered that Jonathan got what he deserved.

During cross-examination, Gamble failed to ask some obvious questions. Since Coleman's friends said Jonathan and Morrisroe had been armed, then where were the weapons now? If other civil rights workers had taken the weapons, then why hadn't they been arrested?

It was hard to believe Gamble wasn't part of Coleman's defense team. He kept referring to "that knife" and "that gun," when talking about Jonathan and Morrisroe, even though the civil rights workers had testified that neither man had a weapon.

The defense attorneys began their closing arguments, holding up Jonathan's blood-soaked shirt and stating that he and Morrisroe were "not men of God as you and I of Alabama know them." They claimed Jonathan wore the clerical clothing to "shield his sinister motive for being in Lowndes County."

"Tom Coleman did as any one of us would have done, protecting that lady there," the attorney told the jury. According to the defense, the killing had nothing to do with Jonathan's urging the black majority in Lowndes County to claim the rights they were entitled to.

Yet part of the defense's statement was true. Coleman was protecting what meant the most to him. It was known as the Southern way of life. It meant denying blacks their rights and keeping the South segregated. Coleman was determined to maintain it. Jonathan was committed to tearing it apart. But Coleman was desperate. So he killed Jonathan Daniels.

Judge Thagard ordered the jurors locked up for the night. As they walked out of the jury box and passed Coleman sitting at the table, the last juror left a telltale sign that was seen by Reverend Morris and others in the courtroom. The juror looked directly at Coleman and winked. It wouldn't be until the next morning, however, that Coleman would learn of his fate and the world would know if justice had been served.

THE VERDICT

By 9 a.m. the following day, jurors were deliberating as Coleman sat in a car with his lawyers in front of the courthouse. After meeting for an hour and twenty-nine minutes, the jurors returned to the courtroom and handed their decision to Coleman's cousin, the district clerk.

She opened the slip of paper, adjusted her eyeglasses, and read the verdict. "We the jury," she began, "find the defendant, Tom Coleman, not guilty."

Jurors take a break at the Confederate monument outside the Lowndes County Courthouse during a recess in the Coleman trial.

Ninety-three-year-old Flora Robinson (left) celebrates with her daughter Cassie Long after registering to vote in Fort Deposit. Robinson's parents had been enslaved in the 1800s. Intimidation had kept her away from Fort Deposit for more than fifty years before she waited in the blazing sun to register in 1965.

Jonathan's Revolution

—Conrad, The Los Angeles Times

'We find the . . . he he he! . . . defendant . . . ho ho! . . . git set! . . . he'ah come the punch line! . . . ho ho! . . . NOT GUILTY!!'

Newspaper
cartoonists from
across the country
expressed their
outrage over the
acquittal of
Tom Coleman.

C ivil rights leaders condemned the "not guilty" verdict. The NAACP called it "a monstrous farce." Newspapers from around the country voiced their outrage.

"The press reports say a trial was held this week in Hayneville," blasted the *Atlanta Constitution*, "but this was in error. No trial was held there within the accepted meaning of the word."

"The evidence mattered but little anyway," wrote Pultizer Prize–winning journalist Jack Nelson, who covered the trial for the *Los Angeles Times*. "What mattered was that the killer was a local white man and his victim a civil rights worker."

The *Birmingham News* echoed Nelson's lament. "When such an individual is killed in the Deep South, there is little chance of a state court conviction."

Outraged Americans questioned why there weren't any blacks or women on Alabama juries. Just as Bloody Sunday had showed the police brutality against African Americans trying to vote, the Coleman trial demonstrated how the Southern justice system did nothing to stop the violence.

SPARKING A CHANGE

ESCRU's Reverend Morris insisted that "the entire proceedings here constitute a miscarriage of justice." Certain that defense attorneys had coached Coleman's friends to give false testimonies, Morris contemplated his next step: a lawsuit that would change the Southern jury system and ensure fairer trials.

We'uns Got Us a Huntin' License!

'Don't shoot 'til you see the whites of their collars'

Systematic exclusion—deliberately keeping blacks and women off jury pools in the South—had gone unchecked by federal officials. Believing that Jonathan's death could spark a change, Morris planned to take action but needed an ally. He found it in attorney Charles Morgan.

After the 1963 killings of those four young girls in the Birmingham bombing, Morgan—a white Alabama native—publicly condemned the injustice. It ruined his career in Alabama. Morgan felt he had nothing to lose professionally and everything to gain ethically by joining Morris's new fight for justice.

Together with Connie Daniels, ESCRU, and a group of black Lowndes County residents, Morgan filed a lawsuit against the Lowndes County jury commissioners. The lawsuit was called *White v. Crook*. (Lowndes County resident Gardenia White was the first person listed among the eleven plaintiffs. The first defendant's name was Bruce Crook, a member of the Lowndes County jury commission. Carlton Perdue and Judge T. Werth Thagard were among the others.)

After more than eighty years of inaction by the federal government, Morgan knew the lawsuit could force the government "into the struggle against the all-white, all-male juries of the Southern Justice System."

Hearing the case in 1966—six months after Jonathan's death—federal judge Frank M. Johnson made another monumental civil rights decision. Johnson ordered the inclusion of blacks on the jury rolls. But he didn't stop there. The Alabama law excluding women from juries was also struck down.

White v. Crook revolutionized the Southern jury system. It happened because of Jonathan Daniels. "He set things in motion," Charles Morgan said about Jonathan's role in the precedent-setting decision. "It was one of the great series of cases which resulted in a transfer of structural power. I think that's pretty important."

Jonathan would have recognized that importance. He'd spent his entire life fighting against injustice. He knew there is always more work to be done, and that we all must participate.

"There are moments of great joy and moments of sorrow," he'd written about his time in the South. "I am called first to be a saint, as we all are. The rest is incidental."

Tuskegee Institute students haul a coffin labeled ALABAMA JUSTICE to protest the acquittal of Tom Coleman. Samuel L. Younge Jr. led the march. Younge was shot to death three months later during a dispute over segregated restrooms.

A Life Continues

Change can come slowly, or it can cascade like an avalanche. Since the death of Jonathan Daniels, the civil rights struggle has continued, with significant breakthroughs and frustrating setbacks.

Though bitterly disappointed by the Coleman verdict, civil rights workers quickly renewed their efforts. Teenagers from Selma and Lowndes County continued to make a difference through nonviolent demonstrations. By the end of 1965, the number of blacks registered to vote in Lowndes County had gone from zero to two thousand—about the same number as registered white voters. Five years later, John Hulett was elected as the county's first African American sheriff.

In Dallas County, residents quickly voted Sheriff Jim Clark out of office, largely because of the new black voters.

The impact that *White v. Crook* had on the Lowndes County jury system was profound, and it sparked dozens of similar lawsuits in other states. That's a huge part of the Jonathan Daniels legacy. There's much more.

Half a century after Jonathan's death, we visited Ruby Sales at the SpiritHouse Project—a diverse, intergenerational organization that works for racial, economic, and social justice. It sponsors a fellowship for college interns in Jonathan's honor.

As founder and director of SpiritHouse, Dr. Sales had just returned from Ferguson, Missouri, where the killing by police of an unarmed black teenager caused significant unrest. She was enthusiastic about the mostly peaceful demonstrations against police brutality that had begun in Ferguson and spread across the country. She said the groundswell of awareness and the outcry for social justice equaled the fervor of 1965, when she was a teenage leader working with Jonathan Daniels in the Deep South.

"Jonathan participated in dismantling segregation," Sales told us. "When I think of him I think of four things:

"Unshakeable in his belief for justice.

"Highly passionate, with a temper.

"Intolerant of fools.

"The willingness to make a connection between what he spouted and what he believed."

Dr. Ruby Sales in 2014

Included among Sales's academic achievements is a degree that Jonathan did not quite attain. She earned a masters of divinity from the Episcopal Divinity School (formerly ETS)—the same school where Jonathan was educated.

Recalling their friendship, Sales said, "Jonathan had never met black people like the black people in the South. I had never met a white person who really cared about what happened to black people or felt any commitment. This was a new journey for us and it gave us hope. It tenderized our hearts."

Ruby Sales is among a long list of people who've been inspired by Jonathan. Children at the Jonathan Daniels School in Keene, New Hampshire, have learned of his passion and sacrifice ever since the school opened in 1968. A stone engraving of his likeness is found on the Human Rights Porch at the National Cathedral in Washington, DC. The film *Here Am I, Send Me: The Journey of Jonathan Daniels* documents Jonathan's life and work. And the annual Monadnock International Film Festival presents the Jonathan Daniels Award to a filmmaker whose work contributes to social consciousness.

Along with his hero, Martin Luther King Jr., Jonathan is one of only two twentieth-century Americans included in the Chapel of Saints and Martyrs in England's Canterbury Cathedral. He is considered a saint in the Episcopal Church and his life is celebrated every August 14, the day of his arrest.

Jonathan has places of honor at VMI; at the Episcopal Divinity School; in Keene and in Selma and in Lowndes County and elsewhere. His name is etched on the Southern Poverty Law Center's Civil Rights Memorial in Montgomery,

Alabama. Scholarships, memorials, and annual celebrations are named for him.

Following his acquittal, Tom Coleman defiantly stated, "I would shoot them both tomorrow." He kept working for the highway department and playing dominoes at the Lowndes County Courthouse. In 1966, Judge Thagard dismissed the charges against Coleman for shooting Richard Morrisroe. Coleman died in 1997.

After he was voted out of office, Sheriff Jim Clark worked as a salesman before being jailed for conspiring to import marijuana. He spent nine months in a federal prison for drug smuggling. Clark died in 2007, shortly after making a statement in defense of his vicious response on Bloody Sunday. "I'd do the same thing today if I had to do it all over again." It's hard to ignore the echoes of Coleman's comment.

Stokely Carmichael, who resisted the lure of violence partly because of Jonathan's influence, ultimately condoned it. He became chairman of SNCC and banned white participation. But after calling for "black power," he was ousted from SNCC and became honorary prime minister of the militant Black Panther Party. Later, he moved to Africa and changed his name to Kwame Ture, working for African unity until his death in 1998. He never forgot his unlikely friendship with Jonathan Daniels, though. On a visit to Keene, New Hampshire, twenty-five years after Jonathan died, Ture noted how wide his friend's influence had been. "He has lived a full life because in death he is still alive."

Reverend Judy Upham, who spent two months with Jonathan in Selma and allowed her red Volkswagen to become a vital source of transportation in the movement, petitioned senators to urge the approval of *White v. Crook*. Ten years after graduating from ETS, she became one of the first women to be ordained in the Episcopal Church and the first female rector at Grace Episcopal Church in Syracuse, New York.

Richard Morrisroe had a long recuperation after being shot by Coleman. He left the priesthood and became an attorney and college professor. He gave his son the name Jonathan. Daniels's childhood friends Bob Perry and Gene Felch both named sons after Jonathan, too.

Throughout their lives, Upham, Morrisroe, Charles Mauldin, and Jimmy Rogers have continued as advocates for human rights, as have so many other courageous people included in this book. Former SNCC chairman John Lewis,

Congressman John Lewis spoke with passion on accepting the Jonathan M. Daniels Humanitarian Award at Virginia Military Institute in 2015.

for example, has served with distinction as a US congressman from Georgia since 1986. Jonathan "gave his life to redeem not just the soul of Alabama, but the soul of a nation," said Lewis, who received the Jonathan Daniels Humanitarian Award from VMI in 2015.

Many of these people were greatly affected by Jonathan Daniels and would attest that his passion, integrity, spirituality, and courage have had a lifelong impact. They fondly remember his sense of humor, his playfulness, his love of the arts, and his occasional recklessness. "He was a very human kind of person," said Reverend Harvel Sanders, who spent countless hours with Jonathan at ETS and in Providence. "I guess like all the saints, he didn't always seem like one."

After five decades of working for social justice, Ruby Sales says, "You can't do this kind of work with hate in your heart." She views Jonathan's life as "a wonderful story of human transformation, of struggle, and how this work not only changed Jonathan's life, but it also changed mine. It made us able to be open to the possibilities in people. To be able to accept that people might come to the table one way but that doesn't mean they'll leave the table the same way." She is grateful that her "optimistic hope about life being a dynamic experience came out of the work that we did together."

Those sentiments were echoed by Connie Daniels, Jonathan's mother. Receiving a humanitarian award for her son in 1966, she told the audience about her own hope. "If I can make a wish this would be it: that if Jon could come back it would be for an America where he and every citizen could sing without irony 'the land of the free and the home of the brave.'"

We relocated to **Keene, New Hampshire, several years ago—a pleasant, walkable college town with a strong sense of history.** One man's name kept popping up; we'd hear him mentioned in lectures or at historical society events, or we'd take note when we drove past the Jonathan Daniels Elementary School. Who was this local hero?

We soon found out. Our next question was: why have we never heard of him? This is a national hero. An inspiration. But outside of Keene and a few pockets where he had a particular impact, Jonathan Daniels isn't known at all. We were determined to tell the world his story.

That story ran deeper than we had first imagined. Jonathan's heroism went far beyond his final, courageous act when he took a bullet to defend a teenage colleague. We discovered that Jonathan played a role in many of the major civil rights events of 1965. The depth of his personality became clear as we interviewed his friends and pored over his letters and essays.

While researching this book, the timeliness of Jonathan's story kept being driven home to us by present-day events. The killings of young, unarmed black men by police in Ferguson, Missouri; Baltimore, Maryland; Cleveland, Ohio; and across the country held frustrating echoes of the civil rights struggles a half century earlier. But those recent deaths and beatings ignited a wave of protests against police brutality and racial profiling. A new generation of teenagers and college-aged students were spurred to action—with a passion and endurance comparable to the Alabama foot soldiers of 1965.

Discovering how a white seminarian had befriended and worked with so many of those foot soldiers seemed to provide a template for better race relations today. We hope Jonathan's dedication to nonviolent protest will help initiate change. It has had a great effect on our own commitment to social justice.

Researching Jonathan's life meant much more than reading about him. We knew we must attend services in Brown Chapel, walk across the Edmund Pettus Bridge, sit in the jail cell where Jonathan spent his final night, and visit the courtroom where the appalling Tom Coleman trial took place. (The trial seemed nearly an inverse of Tom Robinson's trial in *To Kill a Mockingbird:* Robinson would be found guilty no matter what the evidence showed, just as Coleman would be declared innocent.)

We experienced the feel of a mass meeting at events in Selma's Tabernacle Baptist Church and in Brown Chapel. During Selma's fiftieth anniversary Bridge Crossing Jubilee, we were privileged to attend a commemoration at Brown Chapel, where many of today's civil rights leaders gave fiery and uplifting speeches. US attorney general Eric Holder pointed to the church's plaque that honors four activists slain in the Selma area in 1965. Holder told the congregation that voting remains a precious obligation. "Next time you think it's too cold or windy to bother to vote, remember that those people died so you could have that right." The first name on the plaque is Jonathan Myrick Daniels.

Our gratitude begins with filmmaker Larry Benaquist, whose generosity has been the key to much of our research. After he and fellow Keene State College professor Bill Sullivan produced their documentary about Jonathan, others who knew Jonathan came forward with previously unseen collections. Larry helped us access some of that priceless material. We gingerly paged through the journals and notes of Rabbi Harold Saperstein—typed on the back of synagogue stationery—and his files filled with SNCC and ESCRU memorandums. We read letters penned by Judy Upham, offering minute details of Jonathan's days in the South. And we viewed unpublished photographs Jonathan took with his Kodak Instamatic 800 camera. Developed after he was killed, the images made Jonathan even more real to us. And on visits to Selma and Lowndes County, we found many more treasures—most notably the people who knew him.

We thank all who have shared their stories with us, filling in details about Jonathan's life. Geraldine Logan told us much about Jonathan's time in jail. Joyce Parrish O'Neal sat in a pew in Brown Chapel and pointed to the doorway where Jonathan and the northern clergy first entered the church two days after Bloody Sunday. Many others told us of working with Jonathan, protesting with him, laughing at his jokes, and being arrested with him. Through e-mails, phone calls, and numerous chats in living rooms and coffee shops, we heard new stories about Jonathan's childhood from his boyhood friends.

Thanks to Keene State College Mason Library archivists Rodney Obien, Brantley Palmer, and their staff for opening the Jonathan Daniels collection to us (often through numerous snowstorms). And to the Selma Public Library for providing hours of microfilm time so we could read southern newspaper coverage of the events of 1965. Thanks to Alan Rumrill, director of the Historical Society of Cheshire County in Keene, who quickly unearthed crucial material in response to our many requests.

Thanks also to our wonderful and exacting editor, Carolyn P. Yoder, and her team at Calkins Creek, and to our cheerful and supportive agent, Liza Voges.

To all who helped with our research and preparation for this book, we are grateful.

THE EARS HAVE IT
A NOTE ON OUR RESEARCH

So who is **that man in the March on Washington photograph on page 59?** There is always a significant amount of sleuthing involved in nonfiction research, but for this photo, we became detectives.

When Jonathan's lifelong friend Bob Perry discovered the image in 2013, he was certain it was "Jonny." Others had no doubt either, including Jonathan's sister and his girlfriend from high school.

But others were adamant that it couldn't be Jonathan. The man is wearing a priest's collar. Jonathan hadn't yet entered the Episcopal seminary in August 1963 when Finnish student Arto Leino snapped the picture. And even if Jonathan had been a seminarian, there would have been no authorization for him to dress in clerical garb.

There are no names listed on the back of the picture, and Leino did not know who he'd photographed. The image went unnoticed for half a century before Perry found it. It caused an uproar when it was published in the *Keene Sentinel*, with some people claiming it had to be Jonathan, and others saying it couldn't be.

We needed to know the truth. If Jonathan had been standing just a few feet from Martin Luther King Jr. as King delivered his iconic "I Have a Dream" speech, it would foreshadow Jonathan's passionate interest in the civil rights movement two years earlier than previously believed. But Jonathan—an avid writer of letters— apparently never told any of his friends or family that he'd been at the march.

We turned to an expert in facial forensics analysis, who enlarged the photo in question. She compared specific features of the man's face and hair to the same features in a dozen photos of Jonathan that were taken within two years of the March on Washington.

She focused on characteristics such as the crease between the man's eyebrows, the ridge above his lips (known as the philtrum), the shape and angle of the nostrils, and the pronounced angle of the hairline below the temple. In all cases, she found what she said were "striking consistencies."

The clincher was the shape, indentations, and angle of the visible ear. "The ear is in fact a part of the body that can be used as an identifying feature, as no two ears are the same," she reported.

"I have found very strong supporting evidence that, absent a twin sibling, the male individual in the questioned image is in fact

The forensics expert noted the similarities of the prominent brow line; the thick, arching eyebrows; the crease between the eyebrows; and the shape of the eyes in this photo from the March on Washington (above) and these photos of Jonathan taken around the same time.

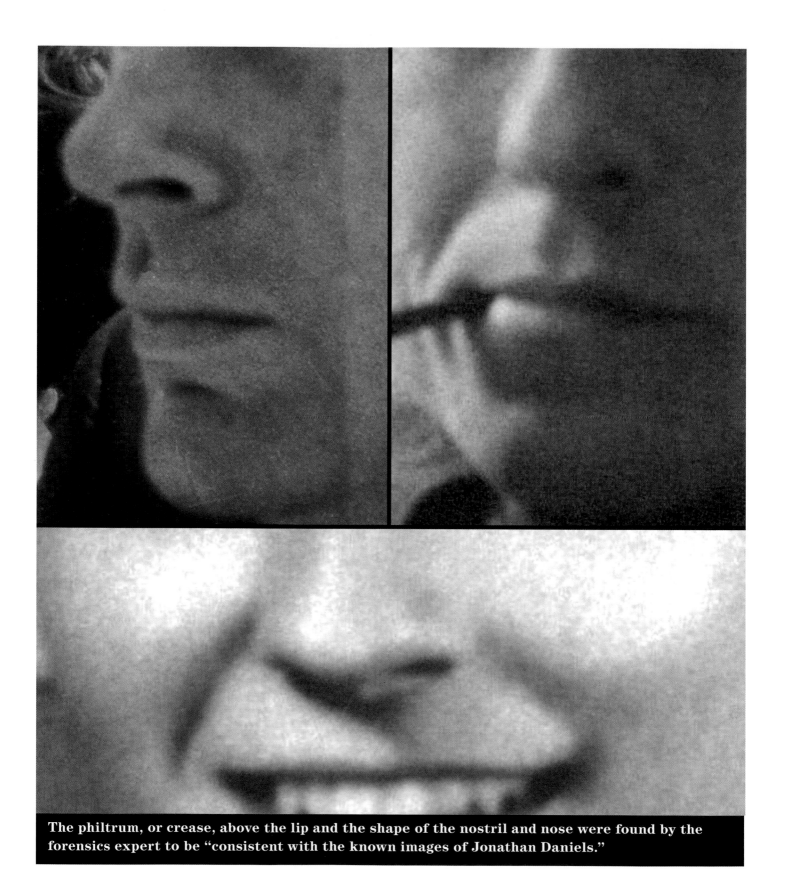

The philtrum, or crease, above the lip and the shape of the nostril and nose were found by the forensics expert to be "consistent with the known images of Jonathan Daniels."

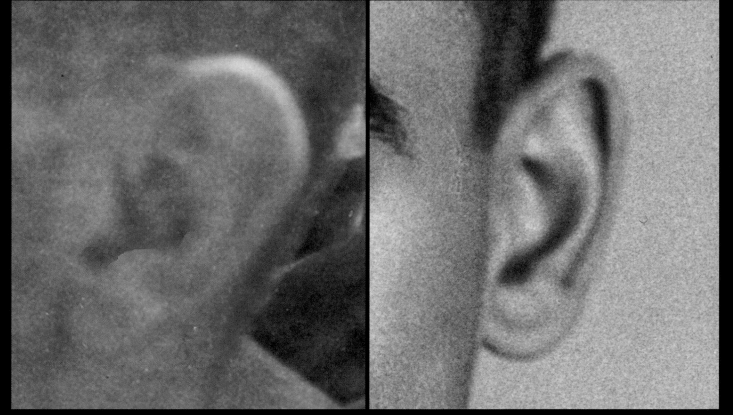

The similarities in the size, shape, and angle of the ear were among many "striking consistencies" noted by the forensics expert regarding the man in the March on Washington photo (left) and several close-up photos of Jonathan. In this pair of photos, attention was paid to the ear canal.

one and the same as the male individual, Jonathan Daniels, viewed in the known images," our expert stated.

Jonathan did not have a twin. We had our proof. Jonathan had attended the March on Washington.

The expert also confirmed that the photo is authentic and has not been altered—a crucial consideration since it is easy to manipulate photographs with today's technology. She stated that the line running through Jonathan's head and the "lighter luminescence" on that side of the image is due to "a change in refraction of the light, possibly due to a glass window."

ANOTHER BIG MARCH

There were other gaps in the Jonathan Daniels story we were determined to fill. Had he marched in President John F. Kennedy's inaugural parade? That was the scene of another monumental speech, when Kennedy called upon Americans to "ask not what your country can do for you—ask what you can do for your country."

As a student leader at VMI, Jonathan would have been likely to march in the inaugural parade with his fellow cadets. But VMI's otherwise efficient record-keepers could not state definitively that he'd been there, as that day's Operations Orders had been lost. After months of dead ends, we turned to the VMI Museum director, Colonel Keith E. Gibson. Impressed with our sleuthing about the March on Washington photo, Colonel Gibson contacted the surviving members of Jonathan's graduating class of 1961, and within hours we had our answer: Jonathan had marched alongside his classmate Doug Popp, who responded to Colonel Gibson's request.

THE FOOT SOLDIERS

The majority of our research for *Blood Brother* came from primary sources. We had access to Jonathan's own words through his years of correspondence, school papers, and tape recordings from his East Selma social work. It became obvious to us that Jonathan's time in Alabama was largely spent working with students who became the backbone of Selma's voting rights movement. One of the most rewarding parts of our research has been connecting with them. They were teenagers in 1965, and they stood with Jonathan at the Berlin Wall, marched with him in civil rights demonstrations, and came to know and respect him. Most had never been interviewed about their experiences with Jonathan.

On trips to Selma, we interviewed former R. B. Hudson High School students Charles Mauldin, Hattie Austin Mays, Ron Fuller, and others. In some cases, our search began with a photo of Jonathan and an unidentified youth in Selma—taken with Jonathan's own camera! But a new friend would identify the teen in the image, then point us in that person's direction. It led to informative, inspiring, and passionate discussions about their days on the front lines with Jonathan. We are honored to publish many of Jonathan's own photos in this book for the first time, alongside images by many of the legendary civil rights photographers.

UNSEEN SOURCES

We were also privileged to have access to primary material from private collections that, in some cases, hadn't seen the light of day in half a century and hadn't been available to previous researchers. Journals kept by Rabbi Harold Saperstein during his dangerous days with Jonathan in Lowndes County provided fresh insight and firm timelines for the final days of Jonathan's life. Saperstein's papers confirmed that Jonathan had a frightening encounter with his killer, Tom Coleman, just days before the murder.

We also viewed a trove of other material in the Keene State College archives, where we spent much of our lives in 2014. The college library's Special Collections room houses two waves of research conducted about Jonathan Daniels. First are the 1966 interviews by the intrepid and unflappable ESCRU founder John Morris, which provided vivid firsthand accounts in the months following Jonathan's murder. Transcripts of interviews done in the 1990s by documentarians Lawrence Benaquist and William Sullivan for their film *Here Am I, Send Me: The Journey of Jonathan Daniels* were invaluable, particularly because many key subjects have died since those interviews were done.

FBI documents and the 303-page Tom Coleman trial transcripts proved chilling and, in the case of the trial transcripts, incomplete. Realizing that the court stenographer had left out information, we filled in the gaps through the stellar newspaper coverage by Jack

While many Alabama clergy chose to wear civilian clothing during civil rights events, Jonathan wore his seminarian collar and ESCRU pin despite the danger.

Nelson of the *Los Angeles Times* and Roy Reed's special reports for the *New York Times*, which was on strike during the trial.

We have accumulated a significant amount of new material, particularly the eighteen fresh interviews we conducted. And since we've built our story in part on work done by earlier researchers, we're "paying it forward" by having our material housed in the Keene State College Mason Library archives, too, as part of that valuable collection.

TIMELINE

KEY EVENTS IN
THE LIFE
AND LEGACY
OF JONATHAN
MYRICK
DANIELS

1939	Born March 20 at Elliot Hospital, Keene, NH.
1939–45	World War II.
1942–43	Lives part-time in Arkansas and Kentucky while his father, Dr. Philip Daniels, trains for military service.
1943	Jonathan's sister, Emily, is born.
1950–53	Korean War.
1954	Supreme Court outlaws segregation in public schools.
1955–75	Vietnam War.
1957	Joins St. James Episcopal Church, Keene.
	Graduates from Keene High School.
	Enrolls at Virginia Military Institute (VMI).
1959	Dr. Philip Daniels dies.
1961	Marches with VMI cadets at John F. Kennedy inaugural.
	Graduates from VMI with honors; elected valedictorian.
	Works in US Senate post office (summer).
	Enrolls in graduate school at Harvard University.
1962	Easter Sunday service inspires Jonathan to enter priesthood.
1963	Attends March on Washington.
	Enrolls at the Episcopal Theological Seminary.
	Becomes member of NAACP.
	Begins fieldwork in Providence, RI.
	President John F. Kennedy is assassinated.
1964	President Lyndon Johnson signs Civil Rights Act into law.
1965	Begins civil rights work in Alabama.
	Participates in Selma-to-Montgomery march.
	Spurs integration of St. Paul's Episcopal Church in Selma, AL.
	Becomes first white civil rights worker in Lowndes County, AL.

	President Johnson signs Voting Rights Act into law.
	Arrested in Fort Deposit, AL, August 14.
	Murdered in Hayneville, AL, August 20.
	Thomas Coleman acquitted of Jonathan's murder.
1966	Because of the Coleman trial, the *White v. Crook* lawsuit successfully challenges exclusion of blacks and women from Alabama juries.
1968	Jonathan Daniels Elementary School opens in Keene, NH.
	Martin Luther King Jr. is assassinated in Memphis, TN.
1980	Jonathan is recognized as a martyr in the Chapel of Saints and Martyrs in England's Canterbury Cathedral. (Martin Luther King Jr. is the only other twentieth-century American with this honor.)
1991	Named a lay saint in the Episcopal Church Calendar.
1997	VMI cadets dedicate a Jonathan Daniels memorial in front of the Lowndes County Courthouse in Hayneville, AL.
2001	Former president Jimmy Carter is presented the first Jonathan Daniels Humanitarian Award from VMI.
2003	Documentary film *Here Am I, Send Me* by Lawrence Benaquist and William Sullivan airs on PBS.
2005	August is declared Jonathan Daniels month by NH governor John Lynch.
2008	Martin Luther King/Jonathan Daniels Committee is founded in Keene, NH, to educate the public about the principles of equality and nonviolence to which they dedicated their lives.
2013	Filmmaker Ken Burns receives the first Jonathan Daniels Award for social consciousness at the Monadnock International Film Festival.
2015	Congressman John Lewis receives Jonathan Daniels Humanitarian Award from VMI.
	Fiftieth anniversary commemorations of Jonathan's death held in Keene and elsewhere.
	Stone carving of Jonathan Daniels added to the Human Rights Porch at the Washington National Cathedral with Mother Teresa, Rosa Parks, and Eleanor Roosevelt.
	Dedications, scholarships, memorial services, lectures, and other events continue to celebrate Jonathan's life.

BIBLIOGRAPHY*

INTERVIEWS

Conducted by Rich Wallace and Sandra Neil Wallace:

Lawrence Benaquist, 2014.

Ronald Fuller, 2015.

Colonel Keith Gibson, 2015.

Paul Johnston, 2015.

Geraldine Logan, 2015.

Augusta Martin, 2015.

Charles Mauldin, 2015.

Hattie A. Martin Mays, 2015.

Richard Morrisroe, 2014.

Joyce Parrish O'Neal, 2014.

Bob Perry, 2014.

Jimmy Rogers, 2014.

Carlton Russell, 2015.

Ruby Sales, 2014.

William J. Schneider, 2015.

Elmira Smith, 2015.

Carolyn Pierce Sturgis, 2015.

Averette Woodson, 2015.

We have also drawn material from interviews conducted by Lawrence Benaquist, William Sullivan, William J. Schneider, John Morris, Howard Mansfield, and others. These are housed in the Keene State College Mason Library Archives and Special Collections, as well as in private collections. Specific references can be found in the Source Notes.

LETTERS

We have drawn on hundreds of personal letters from, to, and about Jonathan Daniels, which are housed in the Keene State College Mason Library Archives and Special Collections; the Historical Society of Cheshire County, New Hampshire; and other collections, including private collections. Specific references can be found in the Source Notes.

*Websites active at time of publication

BOOKS

Branch, Taylor. *At Canaan's Edge: America in the King Years, 1965–68.* New York: Simon & Schuster, 2006.

Carmichael, Stokely, with Ekwueme Michael Thelwell. *Ready for Revolution: The Life and Struggle of Stokely Carmichael.* New York: Scribner, 2003.

Civil Rights Education Project. *Free at Last: A History of the Civil Rights Movement and Those Who Died in the Struggle.* Montgomery, AL: Southern Poverty Law Center, 1989.

Eagles, Charles W. *Outside Agitator: Jon Daniels and the Civil Rights Movement in Alabama.* Tuscaloosa: University of Alabama Press, 2000.

Fager, Charles E. *Selma 1965: The March That Changed the South.* Boston: Beacon Press, 1985.

Frady, Marshall. *Southerners: A Journalist's Odyssey.* New York: New American Library, 1980.

Garrow, David J. *Protest at Selma: Martin Luther King, Jr. and the Voting Rights Act of 1965.* New Haven, CT: Yale University Press, 1978.

Greenberg, Cheryl Lynn. *A Circle of Trust: Remembering SNCC.* New Brunswick, NJ: Rutgers University Press, 1998.

Hampton, Henry, Steve Fayer, and Sarah Flynn. *Voices of Freedom.* New York: Bantam Books, 1990.

Hansberry, Lorraine, Danny Lyon, and Roy DeCarava. *The Movement: Documentary of a Struggle for Equality.* New York: Simon & Schuster, 1964.

Hayman, John. *Bitter Harvest: Richmond Flowers and the Civil Rights Revolution.* Montgomery, AL: Black Belt Press, 1996.

Howlett, Duncan. *No Greater Love: The James Reeb Story.* New York: Harper & Row, 1966.

Jeffries, Hasan Kwame. *Bloody Lowndes: Civil Rights and Black Power in Alabama's Black Belt.* New York: New York University Press, 2009.

Johnson, Lyndon B. *The Vantage Point: Perspectives of the Presidency, 1963–1969.* New York: Holt, Rinehart and Winston, 1971.

King, Martin Luther, Jr. *Stride Toward Freedom.* New York: Ballantine Books, 1958.

Lawson, Steven F. *Black Ballots: Voting Rights in the South, 1944–1969.* New York: Columbia University Press, 1976.

Lewis, John, with Michael D'Orso. *Walking with the Wind: A Memoir of the Movement.* New York: Harcourt Brace & Company, 1998.

Lyon, Danny. *Memories of the Southern Civil Rights Movement.* Chapel Hill: University of North Carolina Press, 1992.

Mendelsohn, Jack. *The Martyrs: Sixteen Who Gave Their Lives for Racial Justice.* New York: Harper & Row, 1966.

Morgan, Charles, Jr. *One Man, One Voice.* New York: Holt, Rinehart and Winston, 1979.

Schneider, William J. *The Jon Daniels Story, with His Letters and Papers.* New York: Seabury Press, 1967.

Stanton, Mary. *From Selma to Sorrow: The Life and Death of Viola Liuzzo.* Athens: University of Georgia Press, 1998.

Vaughn, Wally G., editor. *The Selma Campaign 1963–1965: The Decisive Battle of the Civil Rights Movement.* Dover, MA: The Majority Press, 2006.

Webb, Sheyann, and Rachel West Nelson. *Selma, Lord, Selma: Girlhood Memories of the Civil Rights Days* as told to Frank Sikora. Tuscaloosa: University of Alabama Press, 1980.

Williams, Juan. *Eyes on the Prize: America's Civil Rights Years, 1954–1965*. New York: Penguin Books, 25th anniversary edition, 2013.

FILM and AUDIO

Daniels, Jonathan, and Eugene Pritchett. Tape recordings of interviews with residents of East Selma, 1965.

eFootage.com. "Richmond Flowers Interview at Liuzzo Murder Trial." efootage.com/stock-footage/86553Richmond_Flowers_Interview_At_Luizzo_Murder_Trial.

Here Am I, Send Me: The Journey of Jonathan Daniels. Lawrence Benaquist and William Sullivan. Sojourner Films, 2003.

Morris, John B. *The Saga of Selma: A Tape Recording by ESCRU*, 1965.

The National Archives. "Testimony of John Lewis from a hearing resulting from the March 7, 1965, march from Selma to Montgomery in support of voting rights." archives.gov/exhibits/eyewitness/html.php?section=2.

National Public Radio. "'Segregation Forever': A Fiery Pledge Forgiven, But Not Forgotten." January 10, 2013. npr.org/2013/01/14/169080969/segregation-forever-a-fiery-pledge-forgiven-but-not-forgotten.

Presidential Recordings Program, Miller Center of Public Affairs, University of Virginia. "The Murder of Civil Rights Activist Jonathan Daniels, August 20, 1965." Conversation between President Lyndon B. Johnson and his chief civil rights aide, Lee White. (transcript) whitehousetapes.net.

Washington University Digital Gateway Texts. Judy Richardson interview with Stokely Carmichael, November 7, 1988. digital.wustl.edu.

GOVERNMENT RECORDS

Federal Bureau of Investigation Freedom of Information/Privacy Acts Release: Jonathan Myrick Daniels. 1965.

Johnson, President Lyndon B. "A Special Message to the Congress: The American Promise," March 15, 1965.

Kennedy, President John F. Inaugural Address, January 20, 1961.

McMeans v. Mayor's Court, Fort Deposit, Alabama. U.S. District Court M.D. Alabama, N.D. September 30, 1965.

National Archives. "John Lewis—March from Selma to Montgomery, 'Bloody Sunday,' 1965." archives.gov/exhibits/eyewitness/html.ph?section=2.

Trial transcript: *State of Alabama vs. Tom L. Coleman* in the 2nd Judicial Court of Lowndes County, Alabama. 1965.

White v. Crook Civil Action No. 2263-N, U.S. District Court for the Middle District of Alabama, Northern Division. 1965.

NEWSPAPERS AND MAGAZINES

Adler, Renata. "Letter from Selma." *New Yorker*, April 10, 1965. newyorker.com/magazine/1965/04/10/letter-from-selma.

Associated Press. "Accused Slayer on Juror List." *Los Angeles Times*, September 28, 1965.

———. "Alabama Rights Slaying Acquittal Is Assailed." *Washington Evening Star*, October 1, 1965.

———. "Alabamian Freed in Rights Attack." *New York Times*, September 27, 1966.

———. "Coleman Freed in Rights Killing." *Newsday*, October 1, 1965.

———. "County in Alabama Drops Voting Test Called Harsh." *New York Times*, July 9, 1965.

———. "Indictment Refused in Rights Shooting." *New York Times*, September 14, 1966.

———. "'Is He Dead?'—Mother Gets Sad News." *New York Herald-American*, August 21, 1965.

———. "Keene Student Murdered in Hayneville, Alabama." Jim Knight, *Concord Daily Monitor*, August 21, 1965.

———. "Klan Lawyer Killed in Traffic Crash." *New York Times*, August 21, 1965.

———. "Negroes Overflow Offices of Federal Registrars." *Montgomery Advertiser*, August 11, 1965.

———. "Reaction Given to Federal Vote Registrar Order." *Selma Times-Journal*, August 10, 1965.

———. "Rights Goal: Racial Cases for U.S. Courts." *New York Post*, October 5, 1965.

———. "U.S. Registrars Sign Up 1395 on Third Day in State." *Birmingham Post-Herald*, August 13, 1965.

Atlanta Constitution. "Hayneville Verdict Reinforces Demands to Change Jurisdiction in Such Cases." October 7, 1965.

Baker, Robert E. "Outcry Grows on Coleman Trial." *Washington Post*, October 2, 1965.

Bennett, James. "Alabama Will File Suit Contesting Voting Law." *Birmingham Post-Herald*, August 13, 1965.

Birmingham News. "In Daniels Case: Episcopal Leaders: No License to Kill." October 2, 1965.

———. "The South Has a New Concern." October 1, 1965.

Bloom, Marshall. "Still No One Arrested in Jackson Killing." *Southern Courier*, August 6, 1965.

Blow, Charles M. "This Is Your Moment." *New York Times*, December 10, 2014.

Boston Herald. "Daniels Took Beliefs to South." August 21, 1965.

———. "N.H. Cleric Slain in Ala.; Springfield March Is On." August 21, 1965.

Daniels, Jonathan Myrick. "A Burning Bush." *New Hampshire Churchman*, June 1965.

———. "Inside the Covers." Keene High School *Enterprise*, Spring 1956.

———. "Magnificat in a Minor Key." *New Hampshire Churchman*, October 1965.

———. "On Compulsory Church." *VMI Cadet*, October 2, 1959.

———. "Reality." Keene High School *Enterprise*, Spring 1956.

———. "The Stranger." Keene High School *Enterprise*, Spring 1955.

Detroit News. "Lowndes County Justice." October 1, 1965.

Fenton, John H. "Slain Seminarian Honored at Rites." *New York Times*, August 24, 1965.

Gilbert, Steve. "A Death Breathes Life into a Bygone Era." *Keene* (NH) *Sentinel*, August 2, 2014.

———. "A Man, a Photo, a Mystery." *Keene* (NH) *Sentinel*, April 12, 2015.

———. "Old Photo Offers New Window into Life of Jonathan Daniels." *Keene* (NH) *Sentinel*, August 18, 2013.

Gordon, David M. "Daniels in South to Battle Hatred." *Southern Courier*, August 28–29, 1965.

———. "48 Picketers Arrested in First Fort Deposit March." *Southern Courier*, August 20, 1965.

———. "Selma: Quiet After the Battle." *Southern Courier*, July 23, 1965.

Graham, Fred M. "U.S. Seeks a Case in Rights Death." *New York Times*, October 2, 1965.

Grimes, William. "William A. Price, Journalist Who Defied Senate Panel, Dies at 94." *New York Times*, May 2, 2009.

Heinz, W. C., and Bard Lindeman. "The Meaning of the Selma March: Great Day at Trickem Fork." *Saturday Evening Post*, May 22, 1965.

Herbers, John. "9 Counties to Get Vote Aides Today." *New York Times*, August 10, 1965.

———. "U.S. Mediated Peaceful Confrontation." *New York Times*, March 9, 1965.

Hevesi, Dennis. "Richmond Flowers Is Dead at 88; Challenged Segregation and Klan." *New York Times*, August 11, 2007.

Huie, William Bradford. "Alabama Attorney General Fears for His Life in Court." *New York Herald-Tribune*.

———. "State Attorney Ousted by Rights Trial." *New York Herald-Tribune*, September 29, 1965.

Janson, Donald. "2,000 Guardsmen on Chicago Alert." *New York Times*, August 14, 1965.

Kannerstein, Greg. "Car Wreck Near Tuscaloosa Kills Klan Lawyer Murphy." *Southern Courier*, August 28–29, 1965.

Keene Evening Sentinel. "Civil Rights Dignitaries Honor Slain Seminarian." August 24, 1965.

———. "It WAS his business, as it was His business." August 24, 1965.

Kenworthy, E. W. "Johnson Signs Voting Rights Bill, Orders Immediate Enforcement." *New York Times*, August 6, 1965.

Kupfer, Marvin. "Matt Murphy, Attorney for Klan, Works to Build KKK Membership." *Southern Courier*, July 23, 1965.

Lankford, Tom. "March Turned Back in Eerie Scene." *Birmingham News*, March 8, 1965.

La Rosa, Paul. "Civil Rights Hero Goes from Footnote to Icon." *Episcopal Life*, January 1991.

Los Angeles Times. "Jim Clark, 84; Sheriff Stunned the U.S. with Violent Response to Selma March." June 7, 2007.

———. "Minister Calls Verdict in Hayneville 'Charade.'" October 1, 1965.

Mansfield, Howard. "The Movement's Unheralded Hero." *Washington Post*, November 6, 1990.

McGeorge Law Review. "Voices of the Civil Rights Division." October 28, 2011.

McGrady, Mike. "Why Tom Coleman Went Free." *Newsday*, October 2, 1965.

Montgomery, Paul L. "35 Arrests End Truce in Springfield." *New York Times*, August 15, 1965.

Nelson, Jack. "Alabama Court Charade Cries Out for Intervention." *Los Angeles Times*, October 3, 1965.

———. "Alabama Jury Weighs Rights Slaying Case." *Los Angeles Times*, September 30, 1965.

———. "Coleman Trial Skipped 8 Witnesses for State." *Los Angeles Times*, October 20, 1965.

———. "Jury Acquits Deputy in Rights Death." *Los Angeles Times*, October 1, 1965.

———. "Records Show Coleman Killed Convict in 1959." *Los Angeles Times*, October 15, 1965.

———. "Rights Murder Jurors Worry Over Criticism." *Los Angeles Times*, November 14, 1965.

Newell, Ralph W. "Funeral for Daniels at 1 p.m. on Tuesday." *Keene Evening Sentinel*, August 23, 1965.

Newfield, Jack. "Man, 17 Funerals Are Just Too Many." *Village Voice*, September 16, 1965.

New Hampshire Churchman. "Memorandum on the Case of Jonathan Daniels: Seven New Hampshire Lawyers Make Recommendations for Strengthening the U.S. Criminal Code." June 1966.

New York Post. "Bitter Blasts Follow Ala. Slaying Acquittal." October 1, 1965.

New York Times. "Albert Johnston, 87, Focus of Film on Race." January 28, 1988.

———. "An Extraordinary Trial." October 2, 1965.

———. "The Fight for Civil Rights, Long After Selma." January 19, 2015.

———. "Man in the News: Selma Police Director John Wilson Baker." March 11, 1965.

———. "Murder Unpunished." December 14, 1965.

———. "Negroes Routed in Camden, Ala." April 6, 1965.

———. "Saperstein, Rabbi Harold" (death notice). November 18, 2001.

———. "Slain Civil Rights Worker Honor Graduate of V.M.I." August 22, 1965.

Perrotta, Frank. "Conduct Rites Today for Keene Seminarian." *Manchester Union Leader*, August 24, 1965.

———. "Seminarian Honored by Hundreds." *Manchester Union Leader*, August 25, 1965.

Poppy, John. "Camden, Alabama: Last Summers of a Dreamlike World." *Look*, November 16, 1965.

Powledge, Fred. "Negroes in Selma Flock to Register." *New York Times*, August 11, 1965.

Reed, Doug. "Episcopal Church Is Criticized." *Keene Evening Sentinel*, August 23, 1965.

Reed, Roy. "Deputy Out on Bail in Alabama Killing of Rights Worker." *New York Times*, August 21, 1965.

———. "High Alabama Aide Lays Death to Klan, Assails Police Head." *New York Times*, August 22, 1965.

———. "Negro Students Are Dispersed by Smoke Bombs in Camden, Ala." *New York Times*, April 1, 1965.

———. "1,500 Turned Back." *New York Times*, March 10, 1965.

———. "Selma Protestant Church Integrated for First Time." *New York Times*, March 29, 1965.

———. "266 Apply to Vote as Selma Speeds Registration." *New York Times*, March 2, 1965.

———. "Voter Drive Is Spurred in Alabama." *New York Times*, August 22, 1965.

———. "White Seminarian Slain in Alabama; Deputy Is Charged." *New York Times*, August 21, 1965.

Roberts, Gene. "Voting Officials Sign 1,144 Negroes First Day of Drive." *New York Times*, August 11, 1965.

Robinson, J. Dennis. "The Making of 'Lost Boundaries.'" SeacoastNH.com, 1997.

Rudd, Edward M. "Tense Lowndes Erupts as Minister Is Slain." *Southern Courier*, August 28–29, 1965.

Selma Times-Journal. "Civil Rights Leaders Will Seek Sanction of Court for March." March 8, 1965.

———. "70 Negroes Arrested After Violation of Judge Hare Order." February 5, 1965.

———. "Sylvan Street Demonstration Continues." March 11, 1965.

Shepherd, Jack. "A Worker Hits the Freedom Road." *Look*, November 16, 1965.

Smith, Robert E. "Coleman Tried Among Friends." *Southern Courier*, October 3–4, 1965.

Southern Courier. "Civil Rights Roundup." August 6, 1965.

———. "Compromise Voting Bill Passed by House, Senate." August 6, 1965.

———. "Counties Observe Special 5-Day Registration Period." July 6, 1965.

———. "A final irony was added . . ." October 9–10, 1965 (page 1, no headline).

———. "Lowndes County Justice." October 9–10, 1965.

———. "Senators Kill Wallace's Bill; All-White Jury Frees Wilkins." October 30–31, 1965.

———. "Violence Stalks the South." August 28–29, 1965.

Southern Poverty Law Center. "Martyrs Remembered: Jonathan Daniels." splcenter.org/JonathanDaniels.

Talese, Gay. "The Walk Through Selma." *New York Times*, March 10, 1965.

Time. "Trials: A License to Kill." October 8, 1965.

Thomas, Rex. "Ala. Deputy Bailed in N.H. Clergyman's Slaying." *Boston Sunday Herald*, August 22, 1965.

Thomas, Robert McG., Jr. "Thomas Coleman, 86, Dies; Killed Rights Worker in '65." *New York Times*, June 22, 1997.

United Press International. "Alabamian Deputy Held as Seminarian Killer." August 21, 1965.

———. "Alabamian Indicted in the Slaying of Seminarian." *New York Times*, September 16, 1965.

———. "Charge Cop with Killing Rights Aide." *New York Newsday*, August 21, 1965.

———. "Johnson Wires Condolence Note." *Keene* (NH) *Sentinel*, August 24, 1965.

———. "Jonathan Daniels Called Man with Christian Commitment." *Keene* (NH) *Sentinel*, August 21, 1965.

———. "Keene Theology Student Killed by Shotgun Blast." *Keene* (NH) *Sentinel*, August 21, 1965.

———. "New Rights Death." *Los Angeles Times*, August 21, 1965.

———. "No Reason for Rights Slaying, Priest Says." *Los Angeles Times*, February 17, 1966.

———. "Priest Still Critical: Deputy Free on Bail." *Keene* (NH) *Sentinel*.

———. "The Trial of Hayneville." September 30, 1965.

Wall, Marvin. "The Case of the Armed Seminarian." *Atlanta Constitution*, October 2, 1965.

Washington Post. "Justice in Hayneville." October 1, 1965.

White, William S. "Hayneville Breaks the Heart of Dixie." *Atlanta Constitution*, October 5, 1965.

Woodlief, Wayne. "VMI Classmates Recall Daniels." *Norfolk* (VA) *Ledger-Star*, August 21, 1965.

Wren, Christopher S. "Songs of Freedom." *Look*, November 16, 1965.

Yokley, Eli. "In Ferguson, Push for Criminal Justice Reform Draws Comparisons to '60s Fight for Civil Rights." *New York Times*, January 18, 2015.

PERSONAL VISITS

Brown Chapel, Selma, AL

Church of the Advent, Boston, MA

Dallas County Courthouse, Selma, AL

Fort Deposit, AL

Hayneville, AL

Historical Society of Cheshire County, Keene, NH

Keene Public Library

Keene State College Mason Library

Lowndes County Courthouse, Hayneville, AL

Lowndes County Interpretive Center, National Park Service, White Hall, AL

Lowndes County jail, Hayneville, AL

National Voting Rights Museum, Selma, AL

Selma Interpretive Center, National Park Service, Selma, AL

Selma Public Library

SpiritHouse Project, Atlanta, GA

St. James Episcopal Church, Keene, NH

St. Paul's Episcopal Church, Selma, AL

ADDITIONAL RESOURCES

Braithwaite, William (VMI classmate). "Reminiscences of Jonathan Daniels," March 15, 1966.

Carmichael, Stokely. Address at Episcopal Theological School, 1966.

Christian Peacemaker Teams. "Martin Luther King, Jr.'s Principles of Nonviolence." cpt.org/files/PW%20-%20Principles%20-%20King.pdf.

Civil Rights Movement Veterans Collection. "Oral History/Interview/Conversation Jimmy Rogers, Linda Dehnad, and Bruce Hartford," June 2001. crmvet.org/nars/jimlind1.htm.

Daniels, Jonathan Myrick. Application to Episcopal Theological School, 1963.

———. Application to Virginia Military Institute, 1957.

———. Episcopal Theological School Field Work Evaluation, Bi-Annual Report, December 1963 (re: Providence).

———. "Foreclosure on a Mortgage." Episcopal Theological School, May 31, 1965.

———. Sermon, January 24, 1965. St. James Episcopal Church, Keene, NH.

———. Untitled paper. Episcopal Theological School, June 22, 1965.

———. Virginia Military Institute Valedictory Address, 1961.

Daniels, Jonathan Myrick et al. Statement from ESCRU regarding seating at St. Paul's Episcopal Church, April 29, 1965.

Dunham, Audrea F. Jones, "Boston's 1963 Stay Out for Freedom: Black Revolt in the 'Deep North.'" WGBH Educational Foundation, 2014.

Felch, J. Eugene, IV. Blog post, inspired-celebratinglife.com, March 18, 2013.

Johnson, President Lyndon B. Telegram to Mrs. Philip Daniels, August 23, 1965.

King, Martin Luther, Jr. Address to Episcopal Society for Cultural and Racial Unity Convention, St. Louis, October 12, 1964.

———. Letter to Mrs. Philip Daniels, August 1965.

Lewis, John. Statement on the death of Jonathan Daniels, August 20, 1965.

Morris, John. Statement, September 30, 1965, via ESCRU.

Perry, Robert. "A Walk Through Jonathan Daniels' Keene." City of Keene Jonathan Daniels/Martin Luther King Committee.

Rodman, Rev. Canon Edward. Sermon and discussion. St. James Episcopal Church, Keene, NH, August 10, 2014.

St. James Episcopal Church, Keene, NH. "The Feast of Jonathan Myrick Daniels," August 10, 2014.

Southern Christian Leadership Conference annual report by Martin Luther King, Jr., 1965.

Student Nonviolent Coordinating Committee (SNCC) press releases, August 20 and 21, 1965.

FOR FURTHER INFORMATION*

At the National Cathedral in Washington, DC, Jonathan's likeness is carved in stone in the cathedral's Human Rights Porch.

JONATHAN DANIELS ONLINE (VIDEO AND AUDIO)

Hear Jonathan's 1961 valedictory speech at VMI: digitalcollections.vmi.edu

Watch Congressman John Lewis's 2015 acceptance speech for the Jonathan Daniels Humanitarian Award at VMI: vmi.edu/Content.aspx?id=10737432184

Hear Ruby Sales and Richard Morrisroe discuss Jonathan on Radio Boston: radioboston.wbur.org/2014/08/01/jonathan-daniels

See coverage of Bloody Sunday on History.com: history.com/topics/black-history/civil-rights-movement/videos/bloody-sunday

Watch footage of the Selma-to-Montgomery march on History.com: history.com/topics/black-history/civil-rights-movement/videos/march-from-selma-to-montgomery

See President Lyndon B. Johnson's March 15, 1965, address to Congress about the right to vote: youtube.com/watch?v=MxEauRq1WxQ

Watch *Blood Brother* authors Rich Wallace and Sandra Neil Wallace interview Ruby Sales, Gloria Larry, Richard Morrisroe, Jimmy Rogers, and Judith Upham about their work with Jonathan Daniels: episcopaldigitalnetwork.com/ens/2015/08/27/video-jonathan-daniels-companions-in-alabama-recall-his-life-death

PLACES TO LEARN MORE ABOUT JONATHAN DANIELS AND CIVIL RIGHTS

Birmingham Civil Rights Institute, Birmingham, AL: bcri.org

Civil Rights Movement Veterans: crmvet.org

Episcopal Divinity School: eds.edu/jonathandaniels

Eyes on the Prize (for teachers): pbs.org/wgbh/amex/eyesontheprize/tguide

Historical Society of Cheshire County, Keene, NH: hsccnh.org

International Civil Rights Center & Museum, Greensboro, NC: sitinmovement.org

Jim Crow Museum, Ferris State University: ferris.edu/jimcrow

Keene State College, Mason Library: keene.edu/academics/library

Martin Luther King, Jr. Center for Nonviolent Social Change: thekingcenter.org

National Association for the Advancement of Colored People (NAACP): naacp.org

National Civil Rights Museum, Memphis, TN: civilrightsmuseum.org

National Voting Rights Museum, Selma, AL: nvrmi.com

Selma to Montgomery National Historic Trail: nps.gov/semo

Southern Christian Leadership Conference (SCLC): nationalsclc.org

Southern Courier newspaper archives: southerncourier.org

Southern Poverty Law Center: splcenter.org

SpiritHouse Project: spirithouseproject.org

Teaching Tolerance (Southern Poverty Law Center): splcenter.org/teaching-tolerance

Virginia Military Institute: vmi.edu/jonathandaniels

*Websites active at time of publication

The source of each quotation in this book is indicated below. The citation provides the first words of the quotation and its document source. Most sources are listed in the bibliography. For those not listed, citations are provided here.

The following abbreviations are used:

KSC (Keene State College, Mason Library Archives and Special Collections)

KSC/B (Interviews conducted by Lawrence Benaquist and William Sullivan, included in the Keene State College archives)

WW (Interviews conducted by Rich Wallace and Sandra Neil Wallace)

August 20, 1965 (page 8)

"The food is vile . . .": J. Daniels letter to Connie Daniels, August 17, 1965.

"They kill people . . .": **KSC**, William J. Schneider interview with Reverend Maurice Ouellet, 1966.

"a traitor to . . .": **KSC/B**, J. L. Chestnut interview, undated.

"It didn't feel . . .": **WW**, Ruby Sales interview, 2014.

"a setup": Ibid.

"We were let out . . .": **KSC/B**, Ruby Sales interview, 1990.

Chapter 1 (page 10)

"We got on our hands . . .": **WW**, Bob Perry interview, 2014.

"We had to do it . . .": Ibid.

"Defiant and . . .": **KSC/B**, Connie Daniels interview, 1989.

"sweet and loving . . .": Ibid.

"a great door . . .": Daniels VMI application, 1957.

"exciting tales of . . .": Ibid.

"dreamed beautiful . . .": Ibid.

"don't kneel . . .": **KSC**, Schneider interview with Carlton Russell, 1966.

"wasn't what I would . . .": **KSC/B**, Martha Searle interview, 1994.

"He was swinging . . .": **WW**, Perry interview.

"Millionaires' Row": **KSC/B**, Henry Parkhurst interview, 1991.

"If you were an . . .": **KSC/B**, Searle interview.

"I was from . . .": **KSC/B**, Parkhurst interview.

"liked to be able . . .": Ibid.

"He was not this . . .": **KSC/B**, Emily Daniels Robey interview, 1989.

"Anybody who couldn't . . .": Ibid.

"deep concern for human . . .": Daniels ETS application, 1963.

"a day's work . . .": Ibid.

"to keep an eye . . .": **KSC/B**, Robey interview.

"Jon was able to sit . . .": **KSC/B**, Parkhurst interview.

Chapter 2 (page 22)

"the Moods": Daniels VMI application, 1957.

"reached a climax . . .": Ibid.

"He went up there . . .": **WW**, Perry interview.

"the basic fulfillment . . .": Daniels, "Reality," Keene (NH) High School *Enterprise*, Spring 1956, p. 19.

"Stop, right now . . .": Ibid., p. 20.

"There wasn't a steeple . . .": **KSC/B**, group interview, undated.

"trash": Daniels VMI application, 1957.

"is the flawless expression . . .": Ibid.

"There must be no . . .": Dwight D. Eisenhower, whitehouse.gov.

"Jon was interested . . .": **KSC/B**, Gene Felch interview, 1994.

"You can have . . .": **KSC/B**, Wayne Miskelly interview, undated.

"He was very . . .": **KSC/B**, C. Daniels interview.

"he was girl crazy . . .": Mendelsohn, p. 198.

"I have three places . . .": **KSC/B**, Shirley Fontaine interview, undated.

"to make his peace . . .": Ibid.

"with a terrific thud . . .": **KSC/B**, C. Daniels interview.

"very odd sounds": Ibid.

"in awful agony . . .": Ibid.

"When dawn finally . . .": Daniels VMI application, 1957.

"That really was . . .": **KSC/B**, C. Daniels interview.

"know-it-all": attributed to Reverend. J. Edison Pike, **KSC/B** interview, undated.

Chapter 3 (page 36)

"I knew enough . . .": **KSC/B**, Pike interview.

"helped me immeasurably . . .": Daniels VMI application, 1957.

"I'm not going to . . .": **KSC/B**, Pike interview.

"The whole town . . .": Ibid.

"a lieutenant in the . . .": Daniels VMI application, 1957.

"I think of the South . . .": Ibid.

"all the abuse from . . .": Daniels letter to Gene Felch, October 10, 1957.

"One of my Brother Rats . . .": Ibid.

"At first he assumed . . .": Schneider, p. 16.

"beaten with paddles . . .": Woodlief, August 21, 1965.

"stoop niggers": **KSC/B**, Nolan Pipes interview, undated.

"He called us . . .": **KSC/B**, Felch interview.

"military interference": Daniels ETS application, 1963.

"He hated VMI . . .": **KSC/B**, Felch interview.

"How can he . . .": Daniels, *VMI Cadet*, October 2, 1959.

"commanded respect . . .": **KSC/B**, Major Tom Davis interview, 1989.

"His words were . . .": Schneider, p. 17.

"He could talk . . .": **KSC/B**, Colonel George Roth interview, undated.

"a demanding experience . . ." Daniels, VMI valedictory speech.

"In some colleges . . .": Ibid.

"the metallic click . . .": Ibid.

"The decency and . . .": Ibid.

"shedding false . . .": Eagles, p. 19.

"I have undergone . . .": Daniels letter to Howard A. Reed, May 10, 1962.

"I felt His . . .": Daniels sermon, January 24, 1965.

Chapter 4 (page 54)

"snarling": Daniels letter to Carlton Russell, October 3, 1962.

"The job is beginning . . .": Ibid.

"Each session . . .": Ibid.

"twenty-four-hour job": **KSC/B**, C. Daniels interview.

"I am quick . . ." Daniels ETS application, 1963.

"He came seemingly . . .": Blayney Colmore homily at Episcopal Divinity School, 1990.

"he hit on something . . .": **KSC**, Schneider interview with Colmore, undated.

"I have had a dangerous . . .": Daniels ETS application, 1963.

"looked to me . . .": **KSC/B**, Harvel Sanders interview, 1994.

"challenging, tiring . . .": Daniels ETS evaluation, 1963.

"the remnant . . .": **KSC/B**, Harvel Sanders interview, 1994.

"street language . . .": Ibid.

"the old world had . . .": Ibid.

"The program is . . .": Daniels ETS evaluation, 1963.

"You really didn't . . .": **KSC/B**, Reverend Alan Mason interview, undated.

"Segregation now . . .": quoted by National Public Radio, January 10, 2013.

"self-fulfillment . . .": Daniels ETS application.

"In the long history . . .": President John F. Kennedy Inaugural Address, January 20, 1961.

"We were somehow . . .": **KSC**, Howard Mansfield interview with Blayney Colmore, 1990.

"All of a sudden . . .": Ibid.

"screamed and yelled . . .": **KSC/B**, Reverend Edward Tulis interview, 1993.

"You're walking . . .": Ibid.

"filled with civil rights . . .": Ed Rodman sermon and Q&A, August 10, 2014.

"It is so great . . .": Daniels letter to Mary McNaughton, January 10, 1965.

"quietly frantic": Daniels letter to Carlton and Lorna Russell, October 1964.

"I couldn't ask . . .": Daniels letter to Mary McNaughton, February 9, 1965.

"My rooms resemble . . .": Ibid.

"I'd seen him . . .": **KSC**, Schneider interview with Judy Upham, 1966.

"He was in a . . .": Ibid.

"Gee, I love to . . .": Ibid.

"a very elegant . . .": Daniels letter to Mary McNaughton, March 4, 1965.

"He always held . . .": **KSC**, Schneider interview with Upham.

"I have an uncomfortable . . .": Daniels letter to McNaughton, March 4, 1965.

"bitterly opposed . . .": Daniels ETS application.

Chapter 5 (page 74)

"This demonstration . . .": National Archives: Lewis testimony.

"Can you swim?": **KSC/B**, John Lewis interview, undated.

"No.": Ibid.

"The sight of them . . .": Lewis, p. 345.

"I don't understand . . .": **KSC/B**, Lewis interview.

"My legs fell . . .": Lewis speech at VMI, March 11, 2015.

"call on the clergy . . .": Morris, *The Saga of Selma*.

"He wanted to see . . .": **KSC/B**, Lewis interview.

"There was trouble . . .": Daniels, June 22, 1965.

"I raced back . . .": Ibid.

"I think that's . . .": **KSC/B**, Sanders interview.

"There was plenty to do . . .": Rodman sermon and Q&A, 2014.

"Reluctantly I admitted . . .": Daniels, June 22, 1965.

"I wasn't . . .": **KSC**, Schneider interview with Upham.

"Sometimes the call . . .": Daniels letter to Mary McNaughton, March 29, 1965 (quoting one of his teachers).

"I knew then . . .": Daniels, June 22, 1965.

"Hey! You coming?": **KSC**, Schneider interview with Upham.

"Yes, well . . .": Ibid.

"I never did . . .": Ibid.

"Clark was just . . .": **WW**, Joyce Parrish O'Neal interview, 2014.

"Be prepared to . . .": attributed to **KSC**, Schneider interview with Upham.

"Nobody was really . . .": **KSC**, Schneider interview with Upham.

"They only let us . . .": Ibid.

"Both doors opened . . .": **WW**, O'Neal interview.

"We felt a little . . .": **KSC**, Schneider interview with Upham.

"It demonstrated a . . .": **KSC/B**, Lewis interview.

"help the people . . . ": **KSC/B**, interview with West family, 1990.

"outside agitators . . . ": **KSC/B**, Lewis interview.

Chapter 6 (page 102)

"At the moment . . .": Daniels letter to Mary McNaughton, March 29, 1965.

"We are going to . . .": Fager, p. 112.

"The air crackled . . .": Daniels, June 22, 1965.

"We're going to . . .": **KSC**, Schneider interview with Upham.

"When Jonathan . . .": Webb and Nelson, p. 53.

"I have the haunting . . .": Daniels letter to Mary McNaughton, March 29, 1965.

"Jonathan's presence . . .": **WW**, Hattie A. Martin Mays interview, 2015.

"In a strange way . . .": Daniels letter to Mary McNaughton, March 29, 1965.

"who ate and slept . . .": Daniels, June 22, 1965.

"We weren't accustomed . . .": **KSC/B**, Sheyann Webb interview, 1990.

"He would hold . . .": Webb and Nelson, p. 53.

"Jonathan, get back . . .": attributed to Daniels, June 22, 1965.

"My determination . . .": Daniels, June 22, 1965.

"You're dragging her . . .": Ibid.

"And whose fault . . .": Ibid., attributed.

"We all lit . . .": Ibid.

"I'm not interested . . .": Morris, 1965.

"We are not all . . .": Roy Reed, March 29, 1965.

"What would you . . .": Judy Upham letter, February 24, 1966.

"was a rebel . . .": Carmichael at ETS, 1966.

"I'm tired of hearing . . .": Webb and Nelson, p. 121.

"The point . . .": **WW**, Charles Mauldin interview.

"Jonathan had a . . .": Ibid.

"There were too . . .": **KSC**, Schneider interview with Upham.

"Are we ready to . . .": Ibid.

"It was in a way . . .": Ibid.

Chapter 7 (page 116)

"every ounce of . . .": Johnson, p. 164.

"At times history . . .": President Lyndon B. Johnson address to Congress, March 15, 1965.

"It is wrong . . .": Ibid.

"I could not . . .": Daniels letter to Mary McNaughton, March 29, 1965.

"I've got a car.": **KSC**, Schneider interview with Upham.

"Something had . . ." and "The stakes . . .": Daniels letter to Mary McNaughton, March 29, 1965.

"When I ordered . . .": Daniels, "A Burning Bush."

"White trash . . .": Judith Upham letter, April 3, 1965.

"This is a grim . . .": Daniels letter to Harvel Sanders, April 1, 1965.

"Bring us more . . .": **WW** interview with Ron Fuller, 2015.

"all white and . . .": Ibid.

"Yeah, we're with . . .": **KSC/B**, interview with Kwame Ture (Stokely Carmichael), undated.

"I stood security . . .": J. Daniels letter to C. Daniels, March 26, 1965.

"I think he is . . .": Laura Gallagher letter to Carlton and Lorna Russell, January 30, 1966.

"They would refer . . .": **KSC/B**, John Lewis interview.

"I began to feel . . .": J. Daniels letter to C. Daniels, March 26, 1965.

"The problem is not . . .": Ibid.

"Come and march . . .": Adler, April 10, 1965.

"It was a call . . .": **WW** interview with Charles Mauldin, 2015.

"People lined . . .": Judith Upham letter, April 3, 1965.

"I remember having . . .": **WW**, O'Neal interview.

"He is certainly . . .": J. Daniels letter to C. Daniels, March 26, 1965.

"I pray he doesn't . . .": Daniels letter to Mary McNaughton, April 12, 1965.

"Speed up!": **WW**, Fuller interview, 2015.

"Drive as fast . . .": Ibid.

"Get down": **KSC**, John Morris interview with Morris Samuel, undated.

"Sometimes I think . . .": Daniels letter to Mary McNaughton, April 12, 1965.

Chapter 8 (page 140)

"I've heard of the . . .": **KSC/B**, Lewis interview.

"dialogue committee": **KSC**, Schneider interview with Upham.

"white power structure.": Daniels letter to Mary McNaughton, April 12, 1965.

"*Reverend Mathews . . .*": "Contacts: Members of St. Paul's," Jonathan Daniels and Judith Upham, April 1965, private collection.

"If it weren't . . .": **WW**, Mays interview, 2015.

"the nigger trash . . .": Daniels, "A Burning Bush."

"I must confess . . .": Daniels letter to Harvel Sanders, April 1, 1965.

"super-duper . . .": Daniels letter to Mary McNaughton, April 12, 1965.

"I'm ready to . . .": R. Reed, April 1, 1965.

"'active nonresistance'. . .": Daniels, "Foreclosure on a Mortgage."

"I should gladly . . .": Daniels letter to Mary Thoron, April 15, 1965.

"I saw that the men . . .": Ibid.

Chapter 9 (page 154)

"They called the cops . . .": Daniels letter to Mary McNaughton, April 12, 1965.

"You god-damned scum . . .": Daniels, "A Burning Bush."

"This new expression . . .": Daniels et al., statement from ESCRU, April 29, 1965.

"We rarely entered . . .": Judith Upham letter, April 12, 1965.

"Technically we don't . . .": **KSC/B**, Reverend John Morris interview, 1990.

"You should see me . . . ": Daniels letter to Mary McNaughton, April 12, 1965.

"be symbolically seen": **KSC/B**, Morris interview, 1990.

"Know what he is?": Daniels, "A Burning Bush."

"It is the highest . . .": Ibid.

"economic withdrawal": **WW**, O'Neal interview.

"It wasn't termed . . .": Ibid.

"we can hurt . . .": Ibid.

"As a people . . .": Ibid.

"I'm sorry to say . . .": Daniels letter to Harvel Sanders, April 1, 1965.

"Our Massachusetts . . .": Daniels, "A Burning Bush."

"'troublemakers'": Ibid.

"We moved out . . .": Ibid.

"She had told us . . .": Ibid.

"like a big brother": **KSC/B**, West interview.

"We and the Negro . . .": Daniels letter to Bishop Carpenter, April 21, 1965.

"[She] cupped my face . . .": Daniels, "A Burning Bush."

"I got to know . . .": **KSC/B**, West interview.

"Jon was friendly . . .": Ibid.

"He'd try and integrate . . .": Ibid.

"Sometimes I would . . .": Ibid.

"A hacked up . . .": Daniels letter to Mary McNaughton, April 12, 1965.

"Who's this one?": **KSC/B**, Ture interview.

"What are you doing . . .": Daniels, "A Burning Bush."

"Jon and Judy are . . .": Ibid.

"I'll pick my own . . .": Ibid.

"I explained to him . . .": **KSC/B**, Ture interview.

"The special aspect . . .": Ibid.

"the revolution": Daniels letter to Mary McNaughton, April 12, 1965.

"Sure have gummed up . . .": Daniels letter to Mary McNaughton, May 1, 1965.

"the streets": Daniels letter to William Schneider, May 1, 1965.

"I think I used . . .": Ibid.

"Technically, I haven't . . .": Daniels letter to Mary McNaughton, May 1, 1965.

"No white outsider . . .": Ibid.

"Selma, Alabama, is . . .": Daniels, "A Burning Bush."

Chapter 10 (page 172)

"I don't care if . . .": Judith Upham letter to Jonathan Daniels, June 14, 1965.

"What if you . . .": Historical Society of Cheshire County presentation, Keene, NH, August 20, 2013.

"If I do . . .": Ibid.

"Atlanta's a long . . .": Daniels letter to Mary McNaughton, April 12, 1965.

"You didn't have . . .": **KSC/B**, Lewis interview.

"I trusted him . . .": **KSC/B**, Morris interview, 1990.

"One begins by . . .": Daniels, "Magnificat in a Minor Key," October 1965.

"I realized I was . . .": **KSC**, Marc Oliver address in Keene, NH, 1990.

"Marc, it's so . . .": Ibid.

"I'm in the . . .": Ibid.

"Jesus" . . . : Ibid.

"I'll be right . . .": Ibid.

"This is Jonathan . . .": Daniels and Pritchett.

"Forget about that . . .": Ibid.

"What kind of water . . . :" Ibid.

"Do you think . . .": Ibid.

"No, I don't . . .": Ibid.

"I don't either.": Ibid.

"This interruption is . . .": Ibid.

"Mr. Coleman, he's . . .": Ibid.

"The faith with . . .": Daniels, June 22, 1965.

"We were the type . . .": **KSC/B**, interview with Geraldine Logan, undated.

"The thought of . . .": **KSC/B**, interview with Marc Oliver, undated.

"I was a person . . .": **WW**, Sales interview.

"He understood that . . .": Ibid.

"It was a pragmatic . . .": Ibid.

"picture of the . . .": **KSC/B**, interview with Gloria Larry House, 1990.

"I bought a . . .": Daniels letter to Mary McNaughton, April 12, 1965.

"I may have said . . .": Carmichael, *Ready for Revolution*, p. 467.

Chapter 11 (page 202)

"Downstairs.": **KSC/B**, Oliver interview.

"He was fearless . . .": **KSC**, Howard Mansfield interview with Marc Oliver, 1990.

"We bought a ticket . . .": **KSC/B**, Oliver interview.

"Jon was beginning . . .": **KSC**, John Morris interview with Marc Oliver, 1966.

"no white presence . . .": **KSC**, Mansfield interview with Oliver.

"found within . . .": **KSC**, Morris interview with Oliver.

"The day may come . . .": Ibid.

"Look, if you . . .": **KSC/B**, Ture interview.

"You're a racist.": Ibid.

"Oh, don't hand me . . .": Ibid.

"No, you can . . .": Ibid.

"Of course I can . . .": Ibid.

"So you just want . . .": Ibid.

"All right . . .": Ibid.

"Not the usual . . .": Ibid.

"We were so close . . .": Carmichael at ETS, 1966.

"made us change . . .": **WW**, Sales interview.

"I was totally . . .": Daniels letter to Molly Thoron, April 15, 1965.

"You're riding in . . .": **KSC/B**, Sales interview.

"One of the reasons . . .": **KSC/B**, Ture interview.

"I'm starved most of . . .": Daniels letter to Molly Thoron, April 15, 1965.

"Lowndes County was . . .": **KSC**, Mansfield interview with Oliver.

"The Justice Department's . . .": Julian Bond in the *Southern Courier*, August 6, 1965.

"I'm spending more time . . .": **KSC**, Morris interview with Oliver; Morris reading Daniels letter to Oliver.

"I knew how . . .": **KSC**, Mansfield interview with Oliver.

"If you are white . . .": **KSC/B**, Ture interview.

"I make . . .": **KSC/B**, interview with Rabbi Harold Saperstein, undated.

"He was a good looking . . .": private collection, Rabbi Harold Saperstein papers.

"He spoke to them . . .": Ibid.

"As we pulled up . . .": Ibid.

"a couple miles . . .": Ibid.

"You're a madman.": Ibid.

"The first rule . . .": Ibid.

"Jon was a dangerous . . .": Carmichael at ETS, 1966.

"We lived up . . .": Associated Press, August 10, 1965.

"Everyone was wondering . . .:" Doug Harris letter to Connie Daniels, November 20, 1965.

"My freedom depends . . .": attributed to above.

"Can you fix us . . .": Saperstein papers.

"We entered the . . .": Ibid.

"This is the second . . .": Ibid.

"I registered.": **KSC/B**, Saperstein interview.

Chapter 12 (page 222)

"Everybody was afraid": **KSC/B**, Logan interview.

"Klan is very . . .": Branch, p. 290.

"Jon stood out . . .": Carmichael at ETS, 1966.

"The town looked . . .": Gordon, August 20, 1965.

"There's a lot of . . .": Bill Price, private collection.

"They were sure . . .": **KSC**, John Tillson interview with Gloria Larry, undated.

"As frightened as . . .": **WW**, Sales interview.

"there weren't that many . . .": **KSC**, Schneider interview with David Gordon, 1965.

"You could feel . . .": **WW**, Jimmy Rogers interview, 2014.

"But they didn't . . .": **WW**, Jimmy Rogers telephone interview, April 16, 2015.

"All of a sudden . . .": **KSC/B**, Bill Price interview, 1994.

"I remember looking . . .": **KSC/B**, Logan interview.

"What the hell . . .": **WW**, Rogers interview.

"Exercising our . . .": attributed to J. Daniels, letter to C. Daniels, August 17, 1965.

"You don't have any . . .": J. Daniels letter to C. Daniels, August 17, 1965.

"Groups of whites . . .": Richard Morrisroe letter (quoting John McMeans), February 18, 1980.

"Put them niggers . . .": Ibid.

"The next thing . . .": **WW**, Sales interview.

"We were singing . . .": Ibid.

"If you value . . .": Bill Price, private collection.

"It's you people . . .": Ibid.

Chapter 13 (page 238)

"We heard about . . .": **KSC/B**, Gloria Larry House interview, 1989.

"A rioter with . . .": President Lyndon B. Johnson's statement on Watts riots, 1965.

"I am convinced that . . .": Daniels letter to Mary McNaughton, April 12, 1965.

"Unbelievably foul": Carmichael, *Ready for Revolution*, p. 468.

"The place was . . .": Ibid.

"Stop all that . . .": **WW**, Sales interview.

"There was a terrible . . .": Howard Mansfield interview with Ruby Sales, 1990.

"The food is vile.": J. Daniels letter to C. Daniels, August 17, 1965.

"If you won't eat . . .": **KSC/B**, Reverend Francis Walter interview, undated.

"It was a terrifying . . .": **WW**, Sales interview.

"We are having service . . .": Gordon, August 28–29, 1965.

"We drove them . . .": **WW**, Rogers interview.

"Fever is at . . .": Rudd, August 28–29, 1965.

"so much noise . . .": Rex Thomas, August 22, 1965.

"antagonizing things . . ." and "promoting trouble . . .": **KSC**, transcript of CBS archival footage with Tom Coleman.

"This is the world . . .": **WW**, Sales interview.

Dearest Mum . . .: J. Daniels letter to C. Daniels, August 17, 1965.

"I had to leave . . .": **WW**, Logan interview.

"Fish in a barrel.": **KSC/B**, Walter interview.

"Anybody could have . . .": **KSC**, Mansfield interview with Reverend Henri Stines, 1990.

"It was just like fish . . .": **KSC/B**, Walter interview.

"Hey, man . . .": Ibid.

"He was acting like . . .": Ibid.

"Because I . . .": Ibid.

"Are you bailing . . .": attributed to Mansfield interview with Stines.

"Oh, no, no.": **KSC/B**, Walter interview.

"He absolutely . . .": **KSC**, Mansfield interview with Stines.

"I felt like he . . .": **KSC/B**, Walter interview.

"The whole time . . .": **WW**, Sales interview.

"Jon to some of us . . .": **KSC**, John Morris interview with Richard Morrisroe, 1965.

Chapter 14 (page 254)

"we were so happy . . .": **KSC**, Willie Vaughn (John Tillson group interview), 1965.

"Who signed our . . .": Ibid.

"There was an eerie . . .": **WW**, Sales interview.

"signal": Hayman, p. 224, quoting Richmond Flowers.

"This is government . . .": **KSC**, Willie Vaughn (John Tillson group interview).

"People that you get . . .": **KSC/B**, John Lewis interview.

"We'd been in jail . . .": **KSC**, Mansfield interview with Sales.

"Will you all buy . . .": **KSC**, Ruby Sales (John Tillson group interview).

"there was an ominous . . .": **KSC**, Mansfield interview with Sales.

"We could watch . . .": **WW**, Rogers interview.

"The store is closed.": **KSC,** Ruby Sales (John Tillson group interview).

"Next thing I knew . . .": Ibid.

This is what it's like . . .: **WW**, Sales interview.

"Ruby!": **KSC**, Mansfield interview with Sales.

"I just shot . . .": Southern Poverty Law Center.

"If you don't get . . .": **WW**, Rogers interview.

"This one's dead.": **KSC/B**, Morrisroe interview.

"Jon Daniels is . . .": John Lewis statement, August 20, 1965.

"I walked through . . .": **KSC/B**, Ture interview.

"I'm worried about . . .": **WW**, Perry interview.

"Tom Coleman has . . .": attributed to Perdue, United Press International, August 22, 1965.

"They went down . . .": Roy Reed, "High Alabama Aide . . .", August 22, 1965.

"We're not going . . .": United Press International, August 22, 1965.

"If they'd been . . .": Ibid.

"had a call to . . ." and "was acting in . . .": United Press International in *New York Newsday*, August 21, 1965.

"If this is murder . . .": Associated Press, Jim Knight, "Keene Student Murdered," in *Concord Daily Monitor*, August 21, 1965.

"We ain't going to . . .": Rudd, August 28–29, 1965.

"by commercial . . .": Presidential Recordings Program.

"The train won't . . .": Ibid.

"the sensitivity . . .": Ibid.

"If he had . . .": Ibid.

"and let me . . .": Ibid.

"It's hard to get . . .": **KSC**, Reverend John Morris during his interview with Marc Oliver, 1965.

Chapter 15 (page 270)

"I had never seen . . .": Mabel Carmichael, quoted in Carmichael, *Ready for Revolution*, p. 470.

"I grieve with you . . .": Johnson telegram, August 23, 1965.

"Stokely and the . . .": **KSC/B**, West interview.

"one of the most . . .": Martin Luther King Jr. telegram to Selma Joint Memorial Committee, August 27, 1965.

"I meet a lot . . .": Carmichael at ETS, 1966.

"the wheels of . . .": **KSC**, Mansfield interview with Sales.

"We were set up . . .": **KSC/B**, Sales interview.

"In dying . . .": *Keene* (NH) *Evening Sentinel*, August 24, 1965.

Chapter 16 (page 278)

All of the quotes in this chapter are from the trial transcript (State of Alabama vs. Tom L. Coleman) with the exception of the following:

"Justice and law. . . .": eFootage.com.

"We were all made . . .": **KSC**, Mansfield interview with Sales.

"The prosecution . . .": **WW**, Sales interview.

"Keep your black . . .": Nelson, October 3, 1965.

"There's no hate . . .": Hayman, p. 226.

Chapter 17 (page 292)

All of the quotes in this chapter are from the trial transcript (State of Alabama vs. Tom L. Coleman) with the exception of the following:

"a pep talk . . .": **WW**, Sales interview.

"Never.": **WW**, Rogers interview.

"We knew . . .": Ibid.

"two nigger women . . ." Nelson, September 30, 1965.

"I was deliberately . . .": **WW**, Sales interview.

"The state made . . .": *Los Angeles Times*, October 1, 1965.

"The people who . . .": **KSC**, Mansfield interview with Sales.

"not men of God . . .": Nelson, September 30, 1965.

"shield his sinister . . .": Ibid.

"Tom Coleman did . . .": Ibid.

Chapter 18 (page 304)

"a monstrous farce": *New York Post*, October 1, 1965.

"The press reports . . .": Wall, October 2, 1965.

"The evidence . . .": Nelson, October 3, 1965.

"When such an . . .": *Birmingham News*, October 1, 1965.

"the entire . . .": John Morris statement, September 30, 1965.

"The members of . . .": Hevesi, August 11, 2007.

"into the struggle . . .": Morgan, p. 40.

"He set things . . .": **KSC/B**, Charles Morgan interview, 1993.

"There are moments . . .": Daniels, "A Burning Bush."

"I am called . . .": Daniels to his mother and grandmother Weaver, May 1965.

Epilogue: A Life Continues (page 312)

"Jonathan participated . . .": **WW**, Sales interview.

"Jonathan had never . . .": Ibid.

"I would shoot . . .": CBS archival footage.

"I'd do the same . . .": *Los Angeles Times*, June 7, 2007.

"He has lived . . .": **KSC/B**, Ture interview.

"gave his life . . .": **KSC/B**, Lewis interview.

"He was a very . . .": **KSC/B**, Sanders interview.

"You can't do . . .": **WW**, Sales interview.

"a wonderful story . . .": Ibid.

"If I can make . . .": private collection, Connie Daniels remarks at Chicago ESCRU dinner, February 20, 1966.

The Ears Have It: A Note on Our Research (page 320)

All quotes in this section are from ALH Forensic Video Analysis Ltd.: "Jonathan Daniels Comparison Analysis, Image Analysis Report, April 6, 2015," except for the following:

"ask not what . . .": President John F. Kennedy Inaugural Address, January 20, 1961.

INDEX

PICTURE CREDITS

Bob Adelman: front jacket (top), 102–103, 110–111.

Alabama Department of Archives and History, Montgomery, Alabama/ Jim Peppler, *Southern Courier* Photograph Collection: 66–67, 97, 280–281, 311.

AP Images: 138, 140–141, 150–151.

Lawrence Benaquist: 47.

Cordelia Billingsley: 76.

Used by permission of the Conrad Estate: 306.

Corbis Images: 104–105, 192–193.

crmvet.org/Bruce Hartford: 146, 153, 161, 171, 218.

***The Detroit News*, copyright 1965:** 308.

Dolph Briscoe Center for American History, the University of Texas at Austin/Spider Martin photos: 4–5, 78–79, 80–81, 95.

Courtesy Kevin Eckstrom, Washington National Cathedral: 336.

John J. Fawcett, "Don't shoot 'til you see the whites of their collars," *The Providence Evening Bulletin*, August 25, 1965. Copyright © *The Providence Journal*. Reproduced by permission: 309.

Getty Images: 313.

Getty Images/The Life Images Collection: 118.

Reprinted by arrangement with the Heirs to the Estate of Martin Luther King, Jr., c/o Writers House as agent for the proprietor, New York, New York. © 1965. Dr. Martin Luther King, Jr. © renewed 1993 Coretta Scott King: 275.

Historical Society of Cheshire County, Keene, New Hampshire: 12, 24, 27, 46.

The Image Works: 131.

Courtesy of the Jacob Rader Marcus Center of the American Jewish Archives, Cincinnati, Ohio. AmericanJewishArchives.org: 213.

Jonathan Daniels Collections, Mason Library, Keene State College: front jacket (bottom), 15, 44, 54–55, 60 (top), 63, 64–65, 91, 101, 106–107, 109, 114–115, 116–117, 121, 123, 132–133, 142–143, 156, 158, 163, 165, 179 (right), 184, 188, 222–223, 226–227, 230, 234–235, 236, 245, 254–255, 262, 278–279, 283, 284–285, 290–291, 292–293, 294–295, 302, 321 (bottom left and right), 322 (top right and bottom), 323 (right), 325; Photos by Jonathan Daniels: 87, 145, 154–155, 167, 180, 182, 183, 186, 187; Photos by Douglas Harris: 2, 220; Photos by *Keene Sentinel*: 270–271, 272, 277; Photos by Rabbi Harold Saperstein: 178–179, 201, 215.

Keene High School: 28, 32–33, 35 (top).

Keene Public Library: 10–11, 21, 40.

John A. Kouns: 92–93.

Arto Leino: 6–7, 59, 321 (top), 322 (top left), 323 (left).

Library of Congress, Prints and Photographs Division: LC-U9-10344-12: 56–57; LC-USZ62-127732: 74–75, 83; LC-USZ62-135687: 174; *Look* Magazine, July 1965: 128, 195, 197, 198–199, 200, 209.

The Lyndon Baines Johnson Presidential Library: 202–203, 216–217, 274.

Magnum Photos/Bruce Davidson: 124–125, 135, 194.

Magnum Photos/Danny Lyon: 90, 148–149.

Old Depot Museum, Selma, Alabama: 88–89, 172–173, 190–191.

Bob Perry: 17, 18–19, 34–35.

Bill Price/private collection: 210, 304–305.

Private collection: 164, photo by Jonathan Daniels.

Rabbi Harold Saperstein/private collection: 204, 265, 266, 267.

Stephen Somerstein: 126–127, 136.

Courtesy of the Southern Courier Association/Douglas Harris photo: 242–243.

St. James Episcopal Church, Keene, New Hampshire: 38.

Carolyn Sturgis: 22–23, 30–31.

Virginia Military Institute: 36–37, 43, 50, 69, 316.

Sandra Neil Wallace: 60 (bottom), 159, 224, 238–239, 240, 252, 256.